Memories
of
Swindon

Part of the
Memories
series

The Publishers would like to thank the following companies for supporting the production of this book

Main Sponsor
Blick PLC

Associated Dental Products Limited

Blunsdon House Hotel

Brunel Shopping Centre

The British & Foreign Bible Society

Cheriton Nursing Home Limited

Deacon & Son (Swindon) Limited

Hillier Funeral Service

William Hughes (Swindon) Limited

McArthurglen Designer Outlet Great Western

Monahans Ledbury Martin

Nationwide Building Society

New Zealand Milk (UK) Limited

Raychem Limited

Ridgeway Hospital

First published in Great Britain by True North Books Limited
Units 3 - 5 Heathfield Industrial Park
Elland West Yorkshire
HX5 9AE
Tel. 01422 377977
© Copyright: True North Books Limited 1999

ISBN 1 903204 00 3

Text, design and origination by True North Books Limited
Printed and bound by The Amadeus Press Limited

Memories are made of this

Memories. We all have them: people, places and events, some good and some bad. Our memories of the place where we grew up are usually tucked away in a very special place in our mind. The best are probably connected with our childhood and youth, when we longed to be grown up and paid no attention to adults who told us to enjoy being young, as these were the best years of our lives. We look back now and realise that they were right.

Old photographs bring our memories flooding back - coronations and celebrations; talking pictures, Technicolour and television; the war years, rationing, and the shared hopes and fears which created such a warm community spirit; buying things made of nylon and plastic; fashions which took trouserbottoms and hemlines from drainpipes and mini-skirts to the other

extreme; Doris Day, Acker Bilk, Elvis Presley and the Beatles; the jitterbug, the tango and discos; Ford Populars and Minis; decimalisation. Life changed so much over the years. Some changes were big, some small; some altered our lives in ways we never anticipated. Who in the early days of motoring could have foreseen the motorways and traffic systems of the latter decades of the 20th century? Did any of us realise, when we first saw a computer, what a tremendous impact they would have on our lives? Self-service supermarkets and frozen food made our lives easier - but at the expense of our friendly little corner shops. Nostalgia is always such a mixture of feelings . . . We hope that the collection of pictures in this book will remind you of happy days in bygone eras - and who knows, you might even have been there when one of the photographs was taken!

Contents

Swindon through the years

Every Swindonian will agree that Swindon is a remarkable place. The story of its development will be familiar to most readers: a small rural settlement and market town grew up on the hilltop, in the area still known as Old Town. Much later the New Town was created by Great Western Railway when the company decided, in the 1830s, to make Swindon its base. The Railway Works were built, housing was constructed for the

workers and their families, and Swindon New Town became a thriving industrial centre, which was to remain separate from Old Town for the rest of the century.

The Borough of Swindon was incorporated on 9th November, 1890, making Swindon the largest town in Wiltshire. For another half century the fortunes of the town were closely bound to the fortunes of the GWR; Swindon shared in the glory of the GWR's many successes, and when the Government announced plans to nationalise the railways Swindon shared in the company's fears. However, the town was sufficiently realistic to recognise that it was time to look beyond engineering for its prosperity. Taking advantage of

the growth of the motorway network in the South West, it built up new economies; and although the closure of the Railway Works on 27th March 1986 brought much sadness, representing as it did the end of a great era, Swindon's survival was never in doubt. It was already firmly established as one of the 1980s boom-towns, and had set the trend for growth which has continued ever since.

Memories of Swindon is a collection of photographs dating from the 1920s, when the GWR Works were in full production, right through to the second world war and beyond, when modern Swindon began to take shape. Throughout all these changes, daily life went on against a background of national and world events which affected everyone's lives. Readers who grew up in that period will find pictures of the town of their youth - the streets, the cinemas, the Royal visits, the shops, perhaps even the garage where they bought their first car . . . while younger readers who may be seeing these photographs for the first time will gain an insight into the Swindon of their parents and their grandparents - a different town from that of today, but every bit as great, in its own way!

Around the town centre

Events of the 1930s

MELODY MAKERS
Throughout the 1930s a young American trombonist called Glenn Miller was making his mark in the world of music. By 1939 the Glenn Miller sound was a clear leader in the field; his clean-cut, meticulously executed arrangements of numbers such as 'A String of Pearls' and 'Moonlight Serenade' brought him fame across the world as a big-band leader. During a flight to England from Paris in 1944 Miller's plane disappeared; no wreckage was ever found.

THE WORLD AT LARGE
In India, Gandhi's peaceful protests against British rule were gathering momentum. The Salt Laws were a great bone of contention: forced to buy salt from the British government, thousands of protestors marched to the salt works, intending to take it over in the name of the Indian people. Policemen and guards attacked the marchers, but not one of them fought back. Gandhi, who earned for himself the name 'Mahatma' - Great Soul - was assassinated in 1948.

High Street, Old Town, in another era. The Bell Hotel advertises Usher's ales; Usher's is one of Wiltshire's long-established breweries. Founded in Trowbridge in 1824, it was popular throughout the West Country until it was taken over by Watney in 1960; however, it regained its independence in the early 1990s thanks to a management buy-out from Courage, and Ushers was

able to build up a good name with real-ale drinkers again. Courage, of course, also has a long-standing connection with High Street, having taken over Richard Bowly's North Wiltshire Brewery and operated from there until 1978. This building then became Barclay's Bank, with the inscription Bowly, Brewer being retained

as a historic feature - rather a nice touch. The Bell has changed little, externally at least, and still manages to retain its quiet olde worlde charm in spite of its proximity to the Co-op supermarket, which has taken the place of Skurray's garage, seen beyond The Bell Hotel on this photograph.

We were amused to note that, on the original photograph to which we had access, the number plate of the van parked boldly on the giant No Waiting lettering on the road had been tactfully scratched off - we can assume though that this particular van went to the great scrapyard in the sky long ago, and its driver is now surely safe from prosecution.

At the time, parking in Regent Street had an 'alternate sides on alternate days' arrangement.

Illegal parking had become a serious enough problem to warrant legislation by 1960, and the Road Traffic Act of that year introduced the first fixed penalty parking tickets - with offenders incurring the princely fine of £2.00. A glance

across to Holmes & Lucas on the other side of Regent Street may well start readers singing the jolly little jingle that advertised 'E, K, C, O, television and radio' - remember that one? Further down on the same side, beyond Evans & Co, the former Arcadia Cinema has by the time of this photograph become The Classic. It began its life as a cinema in December 1912 when it opened as the Arcadia Picture Palace, later becoming part of the Classic chain, and like many cinemas it was turned into a bingo hall when the big screen began to lose the battle with the small screen. In August 1974 it was demolished, to be replaced by the rather more prosaic Times Furnishing.

Various clues on this photograph of a semi-deserted Regent Street on a distinctly wet and miserable day lead us to date it at around 1950. A first glance suggested wartime, as the shops appear to have their blackout blinds down and the lady pedalling towards the camera seems to be sporting a WVS-style hat. In fact the furniture shop did not become Courts until 1949; prior to this it had been Bertish's until they moved to Commercial Road in 1948. The Milk Bar on the left began the 40s as Hodson Dairy Milk Bar and ended the decade as the Savoy Milk Bar. Many established Regent Street businesses carried on unchanged through the

Events of the 1930s

SCIENCE AND DISCOVERY
By observing the heavens, astronomers had long believed that there in the constellation of Gemini lay a new planet, so far undiscovered. They began to search for the elusive planet, and a special astronomical camera was built for the purpose. The planet Pluto was discovered by amateur astronomer Clyde Tombaugh in 1930, less than a year later.

WHAT'S ON?
In this heyday of the cinema, horrified audiences were left gasping at the sight of Fay Wray in the clutches of the giant ape in the film 'King Kong', released in 1933. Very different but just as gripping was the gutsy 1939 American Civil War romance 'Gone with the Wind'. Gable's parting words, 'Frankly, my dear, I don't give a damn' went down in history. 1936 - Britain set up the world's first television service - black and white, of course. The Queen's coronation in 1953, the first such ceremony to be televised, did much to popularise television.

ROYAL WATCH
The talking point of the early 1930s was the affair of the Prince of Wales, who later became King Edward VIII, and American divorcee Wallis Simpson. Faced with a choice, Edward gave up his throne for 'the woman I love' and spent the remainder of his life in exile. Many supported him, though they might not have been as keen to do so if they had been aware of his Nazi sympathies, kept strictly under wraps at the time.

decades: indeed, Courts remained here until comparatively recently when it moved out of the town centre. Walkers Jewellers made good use of the conveniently prominent side elevation to announce its presence, while beyond, McIlroy's tower, one of Regent Street's familiar features until it was demolished in 1999, is clearly visible.

Above: Large letters on The Regent remind us how excited everyone was by that new phenomenon, the Talking Picture - or Talkies. The Regent was opened on Monday 16th September 1929 by the Mayor, Councillor George Stevens, and during its first week it showed 'Bulldog Drummond' with Ronald Colman, billed as a 100 per cent talking picture. This was not as silly a claim as its may seem to younger readers, as full soundtracks did not arrive overnight; first came music sequences, then part-talkies, then 100 per cent talkies. The first feature film with any talking at all was The Jazz Singer, starring Al Jolson - who is perhaps best remembered for his rendering of Danny Boy in The Singing Fool, released in 1929. The Jazz Singer came out in 1927 and contained two talking sequences amounting to a total of no more than 354 words. The following year Lights of New York became the first 100 per cent talking feature film. Britain was hard on America's heels: the first all-talking feature made in this country was The Clue of the New Pin, released in 1929, with John Gielgud cast as a villain; Hitchcock's Blackmail, released some six months earlier, was the first British-made talking feature and was billed as 99 per cent talking - perhaps a slight exaggeration as there was sound and music but no talking on the whole of the first reel. The sound for early talkies came on sychronised discs, and when these got out of synch with the picture there would be much loud groaning, whistling and protesting from the audience.

Above right: This photographer has captured a hectic scene here, bustling with pedestrians and traffic going about their business, 1957-style. We see a man carrying

a very large box, and a cyclist performing a rather precarious U-turn in Commercial Road. An Austin A35 is waiting to emerge from Byron Street; anyone who had one of these fuel-efficient little vehicles might remember that they had a huge turning circle - especially compared to more modern cars - which could make trying to park in tight spaces somewhat embarrassing. Behind the A35, the hoarding features an advertisement for long-established local brewery Arkell, which in 1870 was the original proprietor of the Great Western Hotel on Wellington Street (now the Flag & Whistle). As the poster reminds us, the Kingsdown brewery was established in 1843, and since that time has been handed down through many generations of the Arkell family. We believe it to be one of the few breweries in Britain whose shares are still all held by members of the founding family.

Right: Here we move away from Swindon centre. To get your bearings for this photograph of Whitworth Road, place the Rodbourne Arms just off the bottom right-hand corner. It looks rather as though kerbs are being laid - just imagine

Whitworth Road with no pavement today! Now a busy thoroughfare, it used to be a peaceful little road, along which housing steadily built up. This snapshot must date from the 20s, since on the right is the sign for G B Lewis' Post Office, and by 1930 this had been taken over by Dickensons. The numbering of the houses which stood along Whitworth Road at that time had all the makings of a taxi-driver's nightmare; those around the Post Office had names but no numbers, then further along came numbers 1 to 29, then more names, then 1-4 Blomfield Terrace, and then numbers 1 to 10. One imagines that the occupants of the three number 1s must have got to know each other quite well, if only through sorting out all the confused non-locals. However, in 1931 everything was renumbered. Number 1 (one of them) became number 133, the post office

became 275, and so on. Simple - when you got used to it!

Below: The passers-by captured on this shot in September 1961 seem to be averting their eyes from the scene of demolition on the corner of Regent Circus and Commercial Road - though had the hoarding not been there, they might have enjoyed the novelty of being able to stand here and see right the way down Commercial Road. The old number 34 Regent Circus, last occupied by a firm of solicitors and accountants, has gone, and the promised redevelopment, for which tenants are being invited to come forward, will be a more modern affair altogether. Clearly it is the destiny of this site to remain in the financial sector, as it now accommodates a bank and an accountancy practice. The next building along to the right (off the picture) did not share its fate, however; number 36 - the premises of Bishop & Edgingtons, agents for the Rollestone Estates - still stands to tell its tale, and does so with a flourish, some might say, with its ornate red brick facade in excellent condition and proudly bearing the inscription 1891.

Events of the 1930s

HOT OFF THE PRESS
The years of the 1930s saw Adolf Hitler's sickening anti-Jewish campaign echoed in the streets of Britain. On 19th October 1936 Oswald Mosley's 7,000-strong British Union of Fascists clashed head on with thousands of Jews and Communists in London, resulting in 80 people being injured in the ensuing battle. Mosley and his 'blackshirts' later rampaged through the streets beating up Jews and smashing the windows of their businesses.

GETTING AROUND
At the beginning of the decade many believed that the airship was the transport of the future. The R101 airship, however, loaded with thousands of cubic metres of hydrogen, crashed in France on its maiden flight in 1930. Forty-eight passengers and crew lost their lives. In 1937 the Hindenburg burst into flames - the entire disaster caught on camera and described by a distraught reporter. The days of the airship were numbered.

SPORTING CHANCE
In 1939 British racing driver Sir Malcolm Campbell hit the headlines when he captured the world's water-speed record for the third time in 'Bluebird' - all his cars were given the same name. A racing driver who set world speed records both on land and on water, Sir Malcolm established world land-speed records no fewer than nine times. His son Donald went on to set further records, tragically dying in 1967 when his speedboat - also named 'Bluebird' - crashed.

Prior to the incorporation of the Borough of Swindon in 1900, the old and new towns were each run by their own Boards. In 1890 the New Swindon Local Board set about building itself a new £9,000 office building in Regent Circus; this was completed the following year and opened on 21st October. Situated between the two town centres, this imposing edifice was well suited to the role of Town

Hall after 1900. The new municipal borough had the largest population of any town in Wiltshire, with the 1901 census recording 45,006 inhabitants, and its first mayor was George Churchward, manager of the GWR Works. By the 1930s the work of the Council had outgrown the Town Hall, and in 1937 new civic offices were built in Euclid Street. Released from its civic duties, the ex-Town Hall then began to relax and let its hair down a little, becoming home to part of the Library, various arts group and dance studios, and the former corridors of power are now sometimes heard to throb to the sound of feet stepping in time to music.

Some streets are planned and some just grow; a street as straight as this, with such neat rows of housing, can only have been planned. Exeter Street was of course built to accommodate GWR workers. Isambard Kingdom Brunel took the challenges and responsibilities of creating a new community very seriously. He oversaw the building of the residential area himself, planning each stage of the construction of the village carefully, negotiating with the GWR and the contractors, and undertaking the sometimes tricky task of protecting the interests of the workers who were to live in the town whilst remaining within the budgetary constraints imposed by the company. This, together with the need to keep to a strict time schedule, probably explains why the houses in Exeter Street, completed by early 1844, are somewhat plainer than those built earlier on neighbouring Bathampton and Bristol Streets. Brunel succeeded in creating for his workers a Georgian-style village with considerable appeal - poor sanitation and overcrowded conditions notwithstanding. These problems have now been overcome, and sympathetic refurbishment in the 1970s has turned this into a very attractive inner-city area which is a credit to the town - an ideal place to live, as well as a valuable and well-preserved piece of heritage. The buildings are now listed.

Below: This is a 1960s view looking northwards along Princes Street, over Whale Bridge and away from the town centre - rather different from the equivalent view today! Here, the off-licence on the left stands on the corner of Oriel Street; opposite is the Whale pub, on the corner of Medgebury Street, and further towards the camera is the garage of H C Preater Ltd, main dealer for Ford cars and Fordson tractors. Skurray's Town Flour Mill, built in 1893, stood near this spot for many years. Mills were often sited beside canals, which at that time provided the cheapest and most convenient form of transport; the roads of the day were pitted with potholes, making for a bumpy ride, and were a far from ideal way of conveying bulky items. Raw materials could be brought to Skurray's mill smoothly, swiftly and cheaply along the Wiltshire and Berkshire Canal, and finished products could leave the same way. The Mill later became part of H C

Preater's garage. H C Preater became Walter Jackson's, and later Cowie's.

Bottom: At various stages between the early 60s and the time of writing Barkham's disappeared, Islington Furnishing Co Limited ended up as Rudi's cafe-bar, and the college building multiplied. Many readers will remember the building which Empire House replaced as the Empire, though in fact it was called the Queen's Theatre when it first opened in 1898, and became the Empire in 1906. What grand names we gave our places of entertainment - the Arcadia Picture Palace, the Empire, the Palace (on Cricklade Road), the Palladium (Rodbourne), the Electra Palace (Gorse Hill) . . . Their very names promised us an escape into a glittering, magnificent fantasy world for an evening. Who would have dreamed of giving a cinema a name as simple as ABC? Later the Empire did in fact also serve as a cinema - one of the largest around, with seating for over 1,000. The Empire continued to provide entertainment of one form or another for more than half a century, but was finally closed in the mid-50s. Then in 1959 the demolition men closed in on it, and out of the dust and rubble rose a rather different structure. This spot is now dominated by Empire House, built as shops and offices, and Swindon College.

Events of the 1940s

HOT OFF THE PRESS

At the end of World War II in 1945 the Allies had their first sight of the unspeakable horrors of the Nazi extermination camps they had only heard of until then. In January, 4,000 emaciated prisoners more dead than alive were liberated by the Russians from Auschwitz in Poland, where three million people, most of them Jews, were murdered. The following year 23 prominent Nazis faced justice at Nuremberg; 12 of them were sentenced to death for crimes against humanity.

THE WORLD AT LARGE

The desert area of Alamogordo in New Mexico was the scene of the first atomic bomb detonation on July 16, 1945. With an explosive power equal to more than 15,000 tons of TNT, the flash could be seen 180 miles away. President Truman judged that the bomb could secure victory over Japan with far less loss of US lives than a conventional invasion, and on 6th August the first of the new weapons was dropped on Hiroshima. Around 80,000 people died.

ROYAL WATCH

By the end of World War II, the 19-year-old Princess Elizabeth and her distant cousin Lieutenant Philip Mountbatten RN were already in love. The King and Queen approved of Elizabeth's choice of husband, though they realised that she was rather young and had not mixed with many other young men. The engagement announcement was postponed until the Princess had spent four months on tour in Africa. The couple's wedding on 20th November 1947 was a glittering occasion - the first royal pageantry since before the war.

The sweep of the railway towards the top of the picture, and below it the geometrically-planned GWR housing with the church and the park visible to the left, help us situate ourselves. Virtually everything that you can see on this aerial view of Swindon has grown up since the mid 1800s. Victoria Road and Regent Circus, for instance, were built as late as 1888. Swindon Old Town, originally the beginning and end of Swindon, does not even feature in this photograph - High Street is off the bottom right corner. This area of land would have been mainly

green fields, with the line of the canal prominent. The only settlement would have been the hamlet of Upper Eastcott, which consisted of around 20 cottages spread out along the road that connected the hamlet with Old Town, a distance of around half a mile; and a little further north would have been Lower Eastcott Farm with a small collection of dwellings grouped around it. One of the few tracks would have been Fleetway, now Fleet Street, which used to run from a spot south west of the settlement of Westcott towards the North Wilts Canal. It is amazing to consider that without the existence of the canal, the GWR works would almost certainly not have been built here; how different this same aerial photographer's shot might have looked then! And with the Great Western outlet village now situated towards the top left corner, the change goes on . . .

Above: Regent Street and Bridge Street are bustling on this photograph, taken in 1963. Parked outside the National Provincial Bank - which in its modernised form as the NatWest still faces Burton's today - we have a Vauxhall FB Victor or VX490; the two models were virtually indistinguishable from the front. Some FB Victors were unusual in having the gearchange (three forward, one reverse) mounted on the steering column and a pull-out handbrake under the dashboard, an arrangement which allowed them to have a front 'bench' seat running the full width of the car, American-style. This made the car seem very spacious; add to that real leather upholstery and lots of chrome, and the de luxe model was luxury indeed! Behind the FB is a car which everyone will recognise - the Mini, which for many people was THE car of the 60s. Weren't cars more easily recognisable in those days? In 1963 pedestrians and motorists were able to co-exist quite happily in Regent Street, with Leslie Hore-Belisha's great contribution to road safety prominent in the foreground. Pedestrian crossings marked out by studs and yellow beacons were introduced in 1934; the first beacons were made of glass and made a wonderful target for little boys with stones, so the glass beacons were replaced by painted aluminium globes. Crossings got their stripes in 1951, and the beacons became plastic and began to wink in 1952.

The Mini, for many people, was THE car of the 1960s

Below: Cromwell Street, as used to be, featuring Normans furniture shop. On the left as we look towards Regent Street, a car park has been created - though the Mk II Cortina apparently prefers to take its chances on double yellows. The construction at the far end will be new shops and offices in Fleming Way. Our advertisement hoardings on the right are focused firmly on the good things of life - beer and cigarettes. 'People who really know beer take Courage', the poster tells us. The very old-established London brewery of Courage, founded by John Courage in 1787, had after the second world war merged with the Reading-based brewery Simonds, which was popular in Swindon. This was an era when the big breweries were battling to dominate the market, and real ale fans were saddened by the disappearance of many small breweries in the 50s and 60s, although the launch of CAMRA, the Campaign for Real Ale, in 1972, did a lot to re-awaken interest in traditional ale. But still the big breweries keep getting bigger, with Courage now part of the giant Scottish Courage group, having amalgamated with the Scottish & Newcastle Breweries in the mid-1990s.

Bottom: A sunny August day down Commercial Road, in 1967, and shoppers are sauntering along enjoying the weather. A sign of the times is the L-plated Vauxhall HB Viva parked outside what was at the time the Wiltshire School of Motoring. A generation is growing up which takes the motor car for granted. Between 1953 and 1963 the number of cars in the country rose from one car for every twenty-four people to one for every seven, and it continued to rise. Domestic finances in 1967 have become more sophisticated, too; an increasing number of people are paid monthly instead of weekly, and the use of credit cards, loans and what became known as the 'never never' to finance large purchases such as cars has become common practice, sometimes to the disapproval of the older generation of the day. Victoria Finance, a few doors along from the driving school, may well have provided some readers with the wherewithal to buy their first car. Driving schools flourished during the 60s, with passing your test becoming a rite of passage for the younger generation. In fact the driving test, along with L-plates and provisional licences, was first introduced in 1935, initially on a voluntary basis; it then became compulsory, and everybody who had taken out their first driving licence since 1st April 1934 was obliged to take a test. The test fee was initially set at 7/6 (37.5p), but the Driving Test Organisation was so honest that when it discovered it had unintentionally made a profit of £16,000, it reduced the fee.

Wartime

In 1939 Britain's Prime Minister Neville Chamberlain had made his announcement to the waiting people of Britain that '...this country is at war with Germany.' The country rolled up its sleeves and prepared for the inevitable. This war would be different from other wars. This time planes had the ability to fly further and carry a heavier load, and air raids were fully expected. Air raid shelters were obviously going to be needed, and shelters were built on open places across the town.

By the time war was declared an army of volunteers of both sexes had already been recruited to form an Air Raid Protection service. At first ARP personnel were unpaid volunteers but when war broke out in September 1939 they became paid staff. It was their job to patrol specified areas, making sure that no chinks of light broke the blackout restrictions, checking the safety of local residents, being alert for gas attacks, air raids and unexploded bombs. The exceptional work done by Air Raid Wardens in dealing with incendiaries, giving first aid to the injured, helping to rescue victims from their bombed-out properties, clearing away rubble, and a thousand and one other tasks became legendary; during the second world war nearly as many private citizens were killed as troops - and many of them were the gallant ARP wardens.

At the beginning of the war Sir Anthony Eden, Secretary of State for War, appealed in a radio broadcast for men between 17 and 65 to make up a new force, the Local Defence Volunteers, to guard vulnerable points from possible Nazi attack. Within a very short time the first men were putting their names down. At first the new force had to improvise; there were no weapons to spare and men had to rely on sticks, shotguns handed in by local people, and on sheer determination . Weapons and uniforms did not become available for several months.

In July the Local Defence Volunteers was renamed the Home Guard, and by the following year were a force to be reckoned with. Television programmes such as 'Dad's Army' have unfortunately associated the Home Guard with comedy, but in fact they performed much important work. The Guard posted sentries to watch for possible aircraft or parachute landings at likely spots such as disused aerodromes, golf courses on the outskirts of towns, local parks and racecourses. They manned anti-aircraft rocket guns, liaised with other units and with regular troops, set up communications and organised balloon barrages.

Other preparations were hastily made around the town. Place names and other identifying marks were obliterated to confuse the enemy about exactly where they were. Notices went up everywhere giving good advice to citizens on a number of issues. 'Keep Mum - she's not so dumb' warned people to take care what kind of information they passed on, as the person they were speaking to could be an enemy.

Older readers will remember how difficult it was to find certain items in the shops during the war; combs, soap, cosmetics, hairgrips, elastic, buttons, zips - all were virtually impossible to buy as factories that once produced these items had been turned over to war work. Stockings were in short supply, and resourceful women resorted to colouring their legs with gravy browning or with a mixture of sand and water. Beetroot juice was found to be a good substitute for lipstick.

Clothes rationing was introduced in 1941, and everyone had 66 coupons per year. Eleven coupons would buy a dress, and sixteen were needed for a coat. The number of coupons was later reduced to 40 per person. People were required to save material where they could - ladies' hemlines went up considerably, and skirts were not allowed to have lots of pleats. Some found clever ways around the regulations by using materials that were not rationed. Blackout material could be embroidered and made into blouses or skirts, and dyed sugar sacks were turned into curtains.

Above: War had been declared, and every citizen of Britain, young and old, male and female, was called upon to put his or her back into the war effort. Those who did not go into military service of one kind or another worked in factories, dug for victory, gave up their aluminium baths and saucepans, joined organisations and aided in any way they could. These boys were not going to be left out; they might be too young to fight but while there were sandbags to be filled they were going to do their bit to protect their school building. Thousands of sandbags were used during World War II to protect the country and its beautiful civic buildings.

Left: A proud father poses for the camera with his latest arrival. The baby had not arrived from Mars, in fact the 'arrival' was not a baby at all, but an anti-gas attack suit which was compulsory for babies in the United Kingdom during the second world war. An air pump at the side of the suit enabled anxious parents to replenish the supply of air to the precious package inside. It is said that most babies were less than enthusiastic abut the prospect of being encased in the suit - and who could blame them? The picture was taken in 1939. In the event there was never any gas attack on British soil during the course of the second world war.

Both pictures: We believe these photographs of Queen Mary in Swindon to have been taken towards the end of the second world war, when Councillor Drinkwater was Mayor. However, we have been unable to find any official report of the visit. This is not altogether surprising, as Queen Mary spent the war years at Badminton House and often visited places unannounced. In any case, Royal visits during the war received no advance publicity, as for security reasons the movements of members of the Royal family were kept strictly secret as far as possible. Normally the only witnesses would be those taking part in the proceedings and a few casual passers-by who happened to notice that something

was going on and stopped to see what it was; a little crowd of onlookers would gather, but there would be no flags or merrymaking and the occasion would be a solemn one. Royal visits were reported at some length in the newspapers after the event - after all, a Royal visit was potentially an excellent morale-booster for the town, but only if people knew about it! Widowed in 1936, Queen Mary continued to play an active public role. She was a regal and well-respected figure, and no doubt she had a few well-chosen words of encouragement for the young ladies standing there smartly while she inspected the mobile canteen. The donation of a mobile canteen by an ex-pat community

Events of the 1940s

MELODY MAKERS
The songs of radio personalities such as Bing Crosby and Vera Lynn were whistled, sung and hummed everywhere during the 1940s. The 'forces' sweetheart' brought hope to war-torn Britain with 'When the Lights go on Again', while the popular crooner's 'White Christmas' is still played around Christmas time even today. Who can forget songs like 'People Will Say we're in Love', 'Don't Fence Me In', 'Zip-a-dee-doo-dah', and 'Riders in the Sky'?

INVENTION AND TECHNOLOGY
Inspired by quick-drying printers' ink, in 1945 Hungarian journalist Laszlo Biro developed a ballpoint pen which released viscous ink from its own reservoir as the writer moved the pen across the page. An American inventor was working on a similar idea at the same time, but it was Biro's name that stuck. A few years later Baron Bich developed a low cost version of the pen, and the 'Bic' ballpoint went on sale in France in 1953.

SCIENCE AND DISCOVERY
In 1943 Ukrainian-born biochemist Selman Abraham Waksman made a significant discovery. While studying organisms found in soil he discovered an antibiotic (a name Waksman himself coined) which was later found to be the very first effective treatment for tuberculosis. A major killer for thousands of years, even the writings of the ancient Egyptians contain stories of people suffering from tuberculosis. Waksman's development of streptomycin brought him the 1952 Nobel Prize for Medicine.

abroad to a nominated organisation within a British town or city was always a much-appreciated gesture of support. Frequently staffed by volunteers, mobile canteens were despatched to wherever tea and sympathy was needed, and their arrival would be a cheering sight to troops and civilian workers alike, bringing as it did the promise of a hot drink, and a much needed break. The banner proudly tells us that this particular canteen was given to the YMCA by Ceylon. Military-style refreshments seem to have been the order of the day; Queen Mary was also photographed rubbing shoulders with the troops - who include members of the Royal Engineers and the Royal Armoured Corps - in the Forces canteen. Here she appears to be consulting the men before choosing her sandwich (inset).

The date given for this snapshot is July 1934, and the grown-ups' smiles, the children's excited faces and the buckets and spades say it all - they're off to the seaside! The GWR introduced special rail daytrips for railway employees as far back as 1849; these subsequently became full weeks, though holidays were unpaid until 1938. The weather looks promising, though overcoats are much in evidence. Most of the men are dressed formally, and though the ties may come off later in the day, the hats will probably stay on; this was a generation that kept its head covered when it went out. They are of course travelling Third Class; those readers with good memories - or those who are familiar with The Mikado - will know that trains with Third Class carriages used to be known as Parliamentary trains, or Parleys, following an Act passed in 1844 by Gladstone's government, which required railway companies to carry third class passengers in enclosed vehicles with seating at a cost of no more than one penny

On the move

Events of the 1940s

WHAT'S ON?
In wartime Britain few families were without a wireless set. It was the most popular form of entertainment, and programmes such as ITMA, Music While You Work and Workers' Playtime provided the people with an escape from the harsh realities of bombing raids and ration books. In 1946 the BBC introduced the Light Programme, the Home Service and the Third Programme, which gave audiences a wider choice of listening.

GETTING AROUND
October 1948 saw the production of Britain's first new car designs since before the war. The Morris Minor was destined for fame as one of the most popular family cars, while the four-wheel-drive Land Rover answered the need for a British-made off-road vehicle. The country was deeply in the red, however, because of overseas debts incurred during the war. The post-war export drive that followed meant that British drivers had a long wait for their own new car.

per mile. This legislation resulted from an enquiry into a train crash at Sonning on Christmas Eve, 1841, in which third class passengers had been travelling on a goods train in low-sided open wagons, with the inevitable consequences. There is some small consolation to be drawn from the knowledge that lessons in safety really are learned from rail accidents; let us all hope that from here we will progress to improving safety before accidents happen ... But no such sombre thoughts are on the minds of the happy band seen here, and now that they have had their picture taken, they had better climb aboard and grab their seats!

Above: The chap on the left seems to be casting a critical eye over Phase I of the Swindon Bus Station... This photograph is dated August 1967, and the official opening took place on 26th September 1967, so it was all very new indeed. Prior to this, Regent Circus had been the hub of the bus network, with buses loading and unloading there. Swindon had had buses for 40 years, having introduced them in 1927 to cover the places with no tram service; their first batch consisted of single decker, 29-seaters with dual doorways. Buses and trams co-existed until July 1929, when the trams bowed out, with the last tram running on July 11th. That same year double decker buses (Leyland Titan TDIs) appeared on Swindon's streets. Noteworthy bus-related events since then include the acquisition of a number of utility double deckers during the war, built to Government specifications which paid scant regard to creature comforts but provided transport for a population which had absorbed hundreds of evacuees; the introduction of one-man buses on May 4th, 1969 - and woe betide anyone who found themselves first in the queue with only a ten-pound note in their purse! and of course the second phase of the bus station, which was opened on 16th August 1984.

Oh, for the days when you bought your car parking ticket from a real live car park attendant who would smile at you, thank you and give you your change - instead of feeding a machine which impassively swallows your coins, occasionally spitting one out again for no apparent reason, and sullenly grinds out a ticket when you have fed it enough; it has no qualms about keeping the change, and if by some misfortune you don't have enough coins to satisfy its appetite it just glares back at you

unhelpfully. As a nation, we began feeding on-street parking meters in 1958; anyone from Swindon who drove up to London in the summer of that year could have had the privilege of parking at one of the first batch of 625, installed in Mayfair, which became operational on 10th July and cost 6d an hour. This photograph shows the site of the old canal, providing convenient parking for shopping in Regent Street. Car buffs can have fun identifying the models captured by the lens here!

Blick - where every second counts

In spite of its unusual name, Blick is in fact a British company. It derived its name from the Blickensderfer typewriter, which in turn was named after the Dutchman who invented and produced these machines towards the end of the 19th century in Pennsylvania, USA. George C Blickensderfer's invention then came across to this country and was marketed by the Blick Typewriter Co Ltd of Cheapside, London.

The next chapter in the Blick story begins in 1917 when Mr G G Rimington visited the USA in his capacity as Chairman and Managing Director of the Blick Typewriter Co Ltd, and came back with the United Kingdom sales rights of a staff time recording machine called the Follett Time Stamp. This device proved so popular that within a couple of years Mr Rimington had set up a subsidiary company under the name of Blick Time Recording Devices at 174 Grays Inn Road, London. Then in 1920 he made another trip to America, and on this occasion he met with Mr Lowe, a director of National Time Recorders Ltd, a British time recorder manufacturer and came to an

agreement whereby Mr Rimington was to market National machines under the trade name of Blick National in the United Kingdom. Between 1920 and 1937 Blick was to sell nearly 12,000 time recording machines in total; in 1927 it was decided that 'National' should be dropped from the name, and thereafter the machines were re-designed and sold under the name of Blick.

In due course Blick Time Recording Devices at Grays Inn Road came of age, and was separated from its parent the Blick Typewriter Co Ltd and established as an independent enterprise in its own right. And it is the launch of this new venture, Blick Time Recorders Ltd, in May 1922, with a nominal capital of £5,000, which marks the true starting point of today's Company.

The joint Managing Directors of the new company were Mr GG Rimington, Mr J H Foster and Mr F G Marquiss, and in fact all three directors remained in post from the formation of the company in 1922 until the business was sold on, some 24 years later. The company remained at its original premises in 174 Grays Inn Road until 1933, when it moved - all the way to 188 Grays Inn Road!

Above: The early Blickensderfer Typewriter. **Below:** *The early workshop.* **Right:** *An early Blick time recorder.*

Innovation and customer focus - the foundations are laid

As far back as 1932 the directors of Blick were making a practice of working with large influential customers to develop new and innovative time recording equipment. One instance of this was the patented Blick 'Telegraphic' Electric Time Stamp, developed in conjunction with Gents & Co Limited of Leicester, a well-known manufacturer of clocks. This equipment was used to stamp a face-upward imprint on Post Office forms, and was designed to withstand hard and continuous use. Exhaustive testing was carried out for a six month period, and between its launch in 1933 and the outbreak of the second world war, 1,016 such devices were sold to the Post Office and 134 to the South African Government Telecommunications Department.

By the end of the second world war Mr Foster was in his 70s; Mr Marquiss agreed that the time had come to sell, and in early 1946 they put an advertisement in The Financial Times.

On 1st April 1946 Mr Oswald Moor and Mr Rodney Pearson purchased equal shares in Blick. The new

Above right: *The patented Blick Telegraphic electric time stamp.* ***Top:*** *King George 'clocking in'.*

directors decided to introduce a servicing and maintenance structure to support sales, with service branches in the main industrial centres; the first depot was opened in Birmingham in August 1946.

At the end of the 1950s another change was made in the company's trading pattern, and this was the shift of emphasis from sales onto rental. Mr Moor, clearly a mathematical wizard, performed in his head the calculations which ran roughly as follows: By changing the mix from 99 percent outright purchase and 1 percent rental to 80 percent outright purchase and 20 percent rental, net profit would be reduced by 75 percent in the first year but doubled in the second year. Or in other words, rental could be made more attractive for the customer and more profitable for the company. In fact, the government obligingly proceeded to make rental even more attractive as an alternative to capital investment on non-production items, as companies found their working capital being squeezed by high interest rates. As a result the proportion of Blick's rental agreements as opposed to outright sale increased significantly.

Having built up the company from a turnover of £21,000 in 1946 to over £200,000 in 1963, Mr Moor and Mr Pearson sold the business to Dufay Ltd in August of that year. Both directors continued to run the business and were joined by Mr Alan C Elliot, the Managing Director of Dufay, who at

Systems Ltd, which specialised in the rental of small telephone and public address systems, and National Time Recorders Ltd - which of course had been Blick's largest supplier in the early days. With the National acquisition came a factory in Orpington, which was soon closed down, and offices in London, Bristol, Leeds and Glasgow. The following year Blick Time Recorders (Holdings) Ltd changed its name to Blick National Systems Ltd to reflect the acquisition of National Time Recorders Ltd and mark the beginning of a new era for Blick in systems technology.

The Amano Partnership

In 1969 Blick was appointed the United Kingdom distributor for the Amano Corporation of Japan. Amano's products were technologically superior to equivalent machines being sold in the United Kingdom at that time, and in 1971 Blick's Managing Director Mr Whetstone visited Japan to set up a more formal arrangement for distributing Amano products. Amano agreed to make modifications to its equipment to meet United Kingdom requirements and the new products arrived in the United Kingdom the following Spring. This was a significant landmark in Blick's history, as from that point on the company was able to phase out the old National products and replace them with more modern and reliable time recorders. Blick soon became Amano's largest distributor outside Japan, and by 1983 it was selling or renting up to 8,500 Amano units per annum. In the meanwhile Amano had moved into Europe, started its own operation in Brussels in April 1972, but Blick continued to buy from Japan until manufacturing started in Belgium in 1988.

By 1991 Amano was producing more powerful 'intelligent' time recording systems, having over the previous decade changed its manufacturing technology from electro-mechanical to electronic microprocessor-based products, and development has continued along these lines up to the present day.

Top left: Blick celebrated its 25 year association with Amano in 1995 when Mr Alan C Elliot and Mr Y Komoto, the President of the Amano Corporation, together planted a Japanese cherry tree at Blick's new extension to its Head Office in Swindon.
Top right: Mr Alan C Elliot, Chairman, Blick plc.

that time was one of the youngest Managing Directors of any public limited company in the United Kingdom. In 1947 the company crept a little further along Grays Inn Road, this time to number 190, where they had a larger floor space and easier access.

The start of acquisitions

During the next two years Blick acquired British Time Recorders Ltd and Universal Electric Time and Telephone Systems Ltd. These acquisitions brought new products to the Group. By 1965 Dufay had decided to focus its activities on the Paint Industry, and its non-paint interests were to be sold. Mr Alan Elliot, Managing Director of Dufay, suggested to Mr Moor that they should put together a 'management buy-out' proposal to purchase Blick from Dufay - although the term 'management buy-out' did not come into common usage until many years later. The bid was successful; finance was forthcoming from the Industrial and Commercial Finance Corporation (now 3i's plc), and on 30th March 1966 Blick Time Recorders (Holdings) Ltd was incorporated. Over the next twenty years the company grew to become the largest time recorder company in the United Kingdom.

By the time Mr Moor retired some five years later, turnover had risen to £734,000 and the company had 115 employees. Mr Moor's retirement left Mr Elliot with a majority shareholding, and he became Chairman of the Blick Group of companies.

In 1972 Blick made two significant acquisitions which increased its rental income and expanded its interests in the communications business: Internal Telephone and Clock

Blick celebrated its 25 year association with Amano in 1995, and to mark the occasion a Japanese cherry tree was planted by Mr Alan Elliot and Mr Y Komoto, the President of the Amano Corporation. This attractive and appropriate tribute to a long and successful partnership can be seen outside the new extension to Blick's Head Office in Swindon.

The move to Swindon

By the mid 70s preparations were being made to relocate Blick's head office, and this time the move was to take it far away from London which had been its home for more than half a century. The Board had considered three possible locations: London, Milton Keynes and Swindon. The increasing costs of operating in the capital and the heavy urban traffic which hampered distribution made it desirable to move out of London. Milton Keynes was rejected because labour and housing availability at that time was poor; it was also felt that it was not well positioned to provide national coverage for the business because it was on the wrong side of London. So it was decided to move to Bramble Road, Swindon.

The Borough of Swindon was looking for a company that would invest in a prestigious building on Elgin Estate, Bramble Road, and the prospect of housing grants and relocation allowances made Swindon a very attractive proposition. Mr Elliot therefore approached the landlords of the Elgin Estate, London & Leeds Investments Limited, a 75 percent owned subsidiary of Ladbroke Developments, who had bought the land from the Ministry of Defence to develop for industrial use. Following discussions between Mr Elliot and the landlords, a specially-designed five-storey office building and warehouse was constructed and leased to Blick with the option to purchase the freehold, an option which Blick exercised in 1982. In advance of the move the company recruited staff from the Swindon area and arranged training for them in London. The move took place in 1975, with the warehouse being occupied in January and the office building a few months later.

Growth continues

In October 1980 another major supplier, English Clock Systems Ltd, was acquired from Smiths Industries. This company had a substantial customer base in the UK as well as abroad, which provided opportunities for Blick to develop sales in new export markets, particularly South Africa.

Another significant acquisition was ITR International Time Ltd which was acquired from Brown and Jackson plc in 1982. ITR had originally been incorporated in the United Kingdom in 1912 by its American parent company and was a wholly-owned subsidiary of IBM from 1951 to 1962. During that time it was known for a while as IBM United Kingdom Time Systems Ltd before changing its name back to International Time Recording Company Ltd in 1963, and finally becoming ITR International Time Ltd. ITR was Blick's largest acquisition so far, with thousands of installations throughout the United Kingdom. The link with Amano helped to support ITR's large customer base during the transition from traditional time machines to electronic products and later to computerised time and attendance systems.

The acquisition of a number of specialist radio communications companies, the most significant of which was Communications Associates Ltd (which later became Blick Communications Ltd) led to Blick expanding into the business of on-site paging communications. In 1981 Blick Communications Ltd launched Datacall, the world's first on-site alphanumeric pager. This product took the market by surprise, stealing a lead on the competition, and resulted in

Below: *The original Blick building in Swindon.*

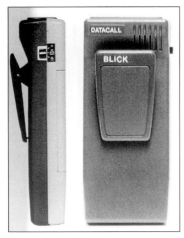

an order from BT worth £750,000 - which set a new record as the largest single order received by the Group. In May 1986 the holding company became Blick plc and obtained a full Stock Exchange listing. At that time the company employed 369 staff and had eight branches throughout the United Kingdom and 15 export distributors. Growth continued the following year with the acquisition of three companies: Thomson & Kelly Ltd in Scotland, Trusound Ltd whose main business was public address, and Yorkshire Telephone Systems Ltd. The new products which came with these acquisitions provided opportunities to develop the communications business, particularly in the areas of door entry, public address and intercom, and the target was to build up a communications rental portfolio that would equal or exceed that of the time products. That objective was achieved in 1992.

In the time and attendance side of the business new products were taking advantage of the latest microprocessor technology and it became clear to the Group that PC-based systems were the key to future developments. In 1988 a company called Programs At Work Ltd was acquired; this eventually became Blick Software Systems Ltd, which was integrated into the Group in 1992. With its own software teams, Blick was now able to work closely with Amano Europe in the development of software for the European Market.

Telefusion Communications Ltd was acquired from the Granada Group in 1991. This company specialised in selling and renting television signal distribution systems mainly to local government authorities; warden call for tenants in council-owned flats and CCTV systems in public areas such as city centres. The Telefusion name was very well known, especially in the TV rental market, and to preserve this association the business was incorporated under the new name of Blick Telefusion Communications Ltd. Two years later Blick Telefusion designed and installed the United Kingdom's first high definition CCTV system in Liverpool City Centre, which has become the blueprint for all city centre installations.

Blick's rental portfolio was further enhanced in 1992 by the purchase of the rights to manage the communication rental portfolio of GPT (an amalgamation of GEC Reliance Systems and Plessey Business Systems). In that same year Blick acquired Electrolay in Northern Ireland. Electrolay had been one of Blick's agents, and had been a distributor of Amano's car parking systems; Amano had wanted Blick to distribute these systems in the UK since 1980. The acquisition of the Electrolay business finally brought car parking into Blick Time Systems Ltd, and the new products integrated well with the Group's CCTV and access control business.

*Above: The world's first on-site alphanumeric pager - Datacall. **Above right:** Public address comes into the Blick portfolio. **Right:** The 'blueprint' CCTV installation in Liverpool City Centre.*

Blick's determination to become a successful rental Group had led it to approach Mercury Communications with a view to purchasing its Time and Security Division, formerly part of Telephone Rentals plc and this major £57 million deal went ahead in November 1993. The biggest acquisition in Blick's history, it doubled the Group's contracted rental income at a stroke, while Time and Security dovetailed perfectly to provide both operating efficiency and opportunities to expand into fresh markets.

For many years the Group had been on the periphery of Security and Access Control, and this finally came within its portfolio in January 1996 through the acquisition of PAC International Ltd, located in Stockport, Cheshire. PAC International was one of the United Kingdom's most successful designers and manufacturers of Security Access Control systems used throughout the world, with a particularly

Above: *An early car parking installation.*
Top: *PAC International Head Office at Stockport, Cheshire.*

strong presence in the USA. This acquisition signalled another major step in the Group's strategy, combining the three key elements - Time Management, On-site Communications and Security. PAC has gone from strength to strength and continues to contribute significantly to the Group's overall performance.

Overseas operation

In 1994 the Blick Group had acquired a small company in France, called Databip, selling radio paging and nursecall products. Two years later Teletechnicon in Holland also became part of the Group; again, this company specialised in supplying paging and nursecall systems to industry and health sectors. These acquisitions were part of Blick's strategy to expand overseas operations to provide distribution points from which to expand into continental Europe. Then in November 1993 Blick seized the opportunity of expanding business into another continent by acquiring TRS (Pty) Ltd in South Africa, a company which had become well known to Blick as a result of the major Mercury Time and Security acquisition. Blick's overseas acquisitions have now been renamed Blick France, Blick Benelux and Blick South Africa respectively.

It would have been difficult for the founders of Blick in 1922 to envisage the growth of their small but thriving enterprise into the successful multinational company that is Blick today. It was the far-sighted wisdom of the current Chairman, Mr Alan Elliot, which enabled the company to exploit the potential for growth based upon a strong rental approach, taking the company from a turnover of £734,000 in 1971 to where it is today: a global organisation with a turnover of £77 million and a gross contracted rental income of £147 million in 1998, employing 1200 people. Blick's association with Swindon is already nearly a quarter

of a century old, and during this period the quality and loyalty of the Swindon people have supported the company in times of rapid expansion, and adapted to meet new challenges.

Today the company boasts an impressive head office, which was extended in 1993 by the addition of 10,000 sq. ft of new offices built by Swindon-based builders E W Beard Ltd. The Group's Chief Executive, Mr Michael Lee, who joined Blick in 1988 as Group Finance Director, has a vision which will take Blick to even greater heights in the next millennium.

Future vision

Blick now supplies on-site support systems and services to industrial, commercial and public organisations, both in the UK and overseas, for the management and security of people at their place of work.

The Group is concentrating its efforts into the core product areas of time and attendance, security and access control and on-site radio communications. With extensive facilities at Stockport and Exeter for research and development and for manufacturing, Blick can offer an exceptionally comprehensive portfolio, which, with the integration opportunities that link the products, effectively makes it a 'one-stop shop' for many of its customers.

Blick will continue to bring new technologies to the market place, offering innovative solutions to the day-to-day business problems of managing people in their working environment. Product development is at the forefront of the Company's activities, and all its products are designed to meet current and future requirements. Commitment to providing sophisticated systems is balanced by a common-

sense approach to their application and use, to make sure that all its products, from the simplest to the most technologically-advanced, are dependable and user-friendly. Customer service and quality have always been a part of the Blick culture, and these concerns are more evident today than ever before. All customers are supported by Customer Care Teams located in Blick Head Office and in the manufacturing sites in Stockport and Exeter.

Within Blick UK Ltd there are 200 engineers in continuous contact with the National Call Centre, which assigns them to regular service and maintenance calls or to emergency callouts where speed of response is critical. Satellite communications are used to pinpoint engineers' positions, identifying the most suitable engineer helping direct them to the job.

Investment in the Group's facilities and staff have resulted in three awards for PAC International: the SWOT Award for Marketing Excellence, North West Business of the Year Award and the 1998 Best Electronics and Electrical Factory

Above left: Mr Michael Lee, Blick's Chief Executive. *Top left:* Blick's impressive new offices when completed in 1994. *Top right:* The 1994 opening of the Swindon Head Office 10,000 sq ft extension. From left to right Mr Simon Coombs then MP for Swindon, Mrs Tara LW Elliot, Deputy Chairman and Mr Alan C Elliot, Chairman. *Bottom left:* Blick Benelux Offices in Holland. *Below:* On-site communications. *Right:* Access control systems.

tions and national and international standards committees ensures all future products meet rapidly changing market requirements.

Sales development is a primary focus and investment in marketing activity, including the establishment of telesales and telemarketing departments in Swindon, supports the experienced sales team. Regular marketing communications to raise brand awareness are a vital part of this activity.

In closing, Blick would like to pass on its thanks, both to its current staff and to those who helped make the company what it is today. The company is very happy to be associated with Swindon and to be a part of the growth of the town. Throughout Blick's history the core values of the Group have remained very much the same: quality, customer service and innovation. Thanks to the commitment of its staff, Blick is now looking forward to the challenges that the next 75 years bring.

Above: State of the art manufacturing.
Top left: *Time and Attendance systems.* ***Left:*** *Service Select national network of service engineers.* ***Below:*** *Blick's national call centre.* ***Bottom:*** *PAC Factory - 1998 Best Electronics and Electrical Factory Award.*

Award, sponsored by Management Today and the Cranfield School Of Management
Staff recruitment and development is the key to Blick's future strategy, and it is adopting the guiding principles of Investors in People. Each and every person in the company has an important role to play in making sure that the business objectives are achieved. A dynamic working environment also features in its plans and is demonstrated by continuous investment in new equipment and office areas to ensure staff can conduct their day-to-day activities efficiently and effectively. Examples of these investments are the new technical engineering workshop in Swindon which tests and repairs customer equipment both old and new, Crowood House, a leased office building off Gipsy Lane, and new regional training and demonstration facilities at the Group's offices in Swindon, Stockport and Exeter.

Quality is not something that can be introduced overnight. It requires an approach to work which has quality built into every level of the structure and procedures. Blick currently has BS EN 9000 quality standards for many parts of its business and aims to apply and extend these standards to all its business activities. Close co-operation with trade associa-

Events & occasions

Above: This night-time shot of the Town Hall, ablaze with patriotic flags, banners, slogans and an illuminated Royal Crown, is a fine sight, but we must confess we find it difficult to be absolutely certain of the date - are we celebrating the coronation of George V in June, 1911? his visit to Swindon in April 1924? or his Silver Jubilee in 1935? or even the Coronation of King George VI in 1937? The classic styling and the solid dignity of Swindon Town Hall remained unaffected by the passing years. The National Anthem, spelled out on the large posters, might equally well be a greeting to a new King or - with the emphasis on Long To Reign Over Us - an expression of loyalty to a reigning monarch. The sentiments expressed on the banners - God Save The King, and One King, One Throne, One Glorious Empire - are equally applicable to any Royal event. And the GR illumination is giving nothing away . . . But the fact is that this ambiguity hardly seems to matter - whatever the occasion, we all welcomed the opportunity to put out the Union Jacks and the banners to show the warmth and depth of our feelings for our monarch, our country and our great traditions. How proud we were to be British!

Right: The engine is No 4082, the Windsor Castle; the month is January, 1936; and the Royal engine, bearing the crowns which we see being affixed to the front, will pull the funeral train of the late lamented King George V from Paddington to Windsor on Tuesday, 28th January. George V had actually driven this train from the Works to the station when he visited the Swindon Works in April 1924, accompanied by Queen Mary. Engine No 4082 was newly built at that time. The next Royal funeral, that of King George VI in 1952, was to pose a tricky problem for the Western Railway, as the Windsor Castle was awaiting overhaul and could not be used. To solve the problem, its plates were transferred to the newer Bristol Castle, No 7013, built in 1948. The substitution was to be permanent, with the No 4082 taking over the identity of No 7013 for the rest of its life - which was a long one, as in fact it survived until 1965.

Events of the 1950s

HOT OFF THE PRESS

The 1950s seemed to be the heyday of spies, and in 1951 the activities of Guy Burgess and Donald Maclean caused a sensation in the country. Both had occupied prominent positions in the Foreign Office, while Burgess had also been a member of MI-6. Recruited by the Russians while at Cambridge University in the 1930s, the traitors provided the Soviets with a huge amount of valuable information. They disappeared in 1951, surfacing in Moscow five years later.

THE WORLD AT LARGE

Plans to develop the economies of member states into one common market came to fruition on 1st January 1958, when the EEC came into operation. The original members were France, Belgium, Luxembourg, The Netherlands, Italy, and West Germany. The Community became highly successful, achieving increased trade and prosperity across Western Europe while at the same time alleviating fear of war which lingered on after the end of World War II. Britain became a member in 1973.

SCIENCE AND DISCOVERY

DNA (deoxyribonucleic acid) was first defined as long ago as 1953, and the effects have been far-reaching. The key discovery was developed over the following years and today DNA fingerprinting has become an accepted part of life. Genetic diseases such as hemophilia and cystic fibrosis have been identified. Criminals are continually detected and brought to justice. Biological drugs have been developed. More controversially, drought and disease-resistant plants have been engineered - and Dolly the sheep has been produced.

Huge crowds have gathered in Regent Circus on 28th April, 1924, to welcome King George V and Queen Mary to Swindon. Arriving at the station shortly after two o'clock, the Royal couple drove straight to the Cenotaph, where they placed a wreath in memory of those who laid down their lives during the first world war. Swindon's official Roll of Honour lists 919 names, although in fact many more citizens are known to have perished. Wartime statistics abound; and although the

accusation is sometimes made that official statistics are meaningless, compiled by people tucked away in offices in an attempt to gloss over the true cost in terms of human suffering, they can nonetheless be an effective way of recording for posterity the sheer enormity of the situation. Before the war 663 Swindon citizens were in the Army and Navy; within two months of the call in 1914, this number had risen to 2,634 - every single one of them an individual with loved ones, responsibilities, and the courage to risk their lives for their country. A total of 5,382 people of Swindon are on record as having served, although again the actual figure was far higher. And when we consider that many of those shown in this picture were, no doubt, included in this total, the statistic becomes very much more meaningful.

Left: Swindon's Cenotaph, photographed on the occasion of the visit of King George V and Queen Mary to Swindon on 28th April 1924, was clearly modelled on the Cenotaph in London's Whitehall. Prior to that a wooden structure had been erected near the old Post Office in Regent Circus in memory of the town's dead heroes, but this temporary measure had proved unpopular with the citizens who, feeling strongly that this was not a fitting tribute, had pressed for a proper monument to be provided at the earliest opportunity. The dignified memorial seen here was unveiled on 30th October 1920. Swindon had indeed acquitted itself honourably during the first world war, with the Victoria Cross, thirteen Distinguished Conduct Medals, nearly twenty Military Medals and around six Military Crosses to its name, in addition to its many valiant sons whose bravery was mentioned in despatches or otherwise officially recognised. Those assembled here were blissfully unaware that only about a quarter of a century would pass before the Cenotaph would be called upon to commemorate those lost in a second world war.

Above: The red carpet is out, and the Royal party is about to emerge from the Town Hall into Regent Circus. In addition to their stop at the Cenotaph, which has drawn immense crowds, their visit to Swindon on the afternoon of April 28th 1924 included a tour of the Victoria Hospital and a tour of the Swindon Works. The Victoria Hospital, built in 1887, had launched a much-needed extension and modernisation scheme in 1912, but work had to be postponed because of the war. Construction finally commenced in October 1922, and the scheme had recently been completed at the time of this photograph. At the other side of town the GWR Works was thriving, with around 1,000 locomotives a year being repaired in the workshops, while the factory had the capacity to build two locomotives a week. The Great Western Railway continued to hit the headlines, having recently claimed another record with its 2.30 train from Cheltenham, which covered the 77.25 miles between Swindon and Paddington in 75 minutes, making an average speed of 61.8 mph from start to stop. The most popular train on its 1924 timetable, however, was said to be the Cornish Riviera Express which left from Paddington at 10.30 every morning and travelled non-stop to Plymouth, a distance of 225.75 miles, taking 247 minutes. This was, apparently, the longest non-stop daily train in the world; and its popularity was due to the fact that it was so comfortable, and so punctual. Did someone say 'those were the days . . .'?

The Baptist Tabernacle forms a dignified backdrop to the 1924 Royal Visit. Much has been written about the architecture of this fine pillared building which in fact stood for less than a century, having been erected in 1886 and demolished in 1978. Suffice it to say here that its classical lines were admirably suited to the formality of occasions such as this. Swindon has enjoyed its share of Royal visits, and one particular Royal connection via the Great Western Railway can be traced back to 13th June 1842, when Queen Victoria became the first British monarch to travel by train; she and Albert went from Slough to Paddington in a 21-foot-long four-

Events of the 1950s

MELODY MAKERS
Few teenage girls could resist the blatant sex-appeal of 'Elvis the Pelvis', though their parents were scandalised at the moody Presley's provocatively gyrating hips. The singer took America and Britain by storm with such hits as 'Jailhouse Rock', 'All Shook Up' and 'Blue Suede Shoes'. The rhythms of Bill Haley and his Comets, Buddy Holly, Chuck Berry, and Roy Orbison (who had a phenomenal three-octave voice) turned the 1950s into the Rock 'n' Roll years.

INVENTION AND TECHNOLOGY
Until the late 1950s you did not carry radios around with you. Radios were listened to at home, plugged into a mains socket in every average sitting room. Japan was in the forefront of electronic developments even then, and in 1957 the Japanese company Sony introduced the world's very first all-transistor radio - an item of new technology that was small enough to fit into your pocket. The major consumer product caught on fast - particularly with teenage listeners.

ROYAL WATCH
King George VI's health had been causing problems since 1948, when he developed thrombosis. In 1951 the King - always a heavy smoker - became ill again, and was eventually found to be suffering from lung cancer. His left lung was removed in September of 1951. In January 1952 he waved Princess Elizabeth and Prince Philip off on their tour of Africa; they were never to see him again. The King died on 5th February 1952.

wheeler called The Royal Saloon, constructed by GWR some while earlier in anticipation of the occasion, and fitted with wooden tyres to deaden the noise. The locomotive, Phlegethon, was driven by Daniel Gooch, with Brunel himself assisting. Queen Victoria was sufficiently amused by the experience to become a frequent rail traveller, although she disliked excessive speed and never allowed her train to exceed 40 mph.

Not really the right weather to step out of Burton's wearing a brand-new suit, with water, water everywhere and passing traffic making huge waves! Montague Burton's good quality menswear has been a firm favourite with the gentlemen for many generations, and the chain grew until virtually every town and city in Britain had at least one branch. The story goes that when soldiers were demobbed after military service they were given vouchers to be fitted out in civvies at Burton's. They went along to the nearest branch and were kitted out in what was then termed 'the full Monty' - and that is the origin of the phrase which has in recent years come to mean something very different from a full suit of clothes! Burton's had two branches in Swindon for a while, one in Bridge Street, with a billiard hall above it, and one in Regent Street. The Bridge Street corner spot pictured here had, in an earlier era when the junction of Bridge Street and Fleet Street was Swindon's Tram Centre, been the site of the Oxford Hotel, which was demolished in the 1930s.

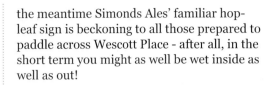

Below: With so much water all around, The Ship is certainly in its element - and the traffic islands really are islands! When Swindon's roads are suddenly turned into rivers, boats seem the best option, so full marks to the enterprising pupils at Headlands School in Cricklade Road whose journey to school by canoe during the floods of July 1968 got a mention in the local newspaper. Fortunately, scenes like this are less common in Swindon these days; records show that in the early decades of the 20th century, heavy thunderstorms regularly caused Cromwell Street (which ran between Commercial Road and Regent Street, where the Brunel development now stands) to flood, but this problem was overcome when the drainage was improved. Flooding certainly makes for dramatic photographs, but for those affected it means a lot of mess and inconvenience, and the cleaning-up operations can drag on for months. But in the meantime Simonds Ales' familiar hop-leaf sign is beckoning to all those prepared to paddle across Wescott Place - after all, in the short term you might as well be wet inside as well as out!

Bottom: Will it or won't it? The chap in the foreground and the spectator looking out of the upstairs window are apparently waiting to see whether the bus will manage to ford the flood in Wescott Place . . . Photographs of Swindon under inches of flood water will bring back memories for many of us of wading through the streets - although probably the most severe floods in recent memory are those which followed the torrential rainfall of 10th July, 1968, when literally gallons of rain drenched the Swindon area. Some four inches of rain fell during the day, but the worst storms came at around 8.30 pm. Thousands of people found their homes waist-high in water; the less fortunate did not manage to get home at all and were stranded in their cars as roads became impassable - among them the dual carriageway of Queen's Drive, which was completely under water and had to be closed. Rail services were disrupted, too; the line was flooded between Swindon and Wootton Bassett, and one consequence of this was that the Royal Mail train going from Paddington to Bristol was stranded at Swindon. It spent the night in a siding, and a police guard had to be mounted to watch over it until it could resume its journey.

Below: Here we see the Town Hall decorated for the Coronation of Elizabeth II in 1953. It was the third Coronation that the nation had celebrated in just over 30 years, but that certainly did not mean that Swindon celebrated with any less enthusiasm; our new monarch had already won our hearts as Princess Elizabeth, and we were proud to have her as our Queen. This Coronation was rather special in that it was the first one to be televised, and for many people this occasion provided them with their very first experience of watching TV. There was something truly thrilling about being able to watch such a historic event as it happened - even if the picture was small and rather flickery - rather than waiting to see the photographs in the paper the next day and watching it on the next newsreel at the cinema; so anyone who had a television set was likely to find the whole street trying to squeeze into their front room!

Right: The City of Truro is one of the great GWR engines to have survived to enjoy a well-earned semi-retirement, and can be seen today in immaculate condition. Built in 1903,

the City of Truro's claim to fame is a speed of 102.3 mph, reported to have been achieved on 9 May 1904 going down Wellington bank, on an Ocean Liner Mails Special from Plymouth. This speed was calculated from the recorded times at which the mileposts were passed, and is disputed by some who claim that one of the times was logged incorrectly. In any event, City of Truro was a fine locomotive; it was withdrawn in 1931, and returned to service in 1957, having spent the intervening years in the old York Railway Museum. Here it appears to be in green unlined livery, and it is thought the photograph was taken on its return from York to Swindon in 1957. In 1961 it underwent restoration, and since then has made a number of appearances, which include taking part in 150th anniversary celebrations of the GWR, representing British steam at the Netherlands Railways 150th anniversary celebrations, featuring in the National Railway Museum on Tour event in 1990, and running various Specials. Seen here bearing the number 3717, City of Truro's glorious 102.3 mph - if correct - was achieved under its original number, No 3440.

Main picture: Certainly a day to remember for these smart little chaps, especially the ones in the front row who were just inches away from HRH The Princess Elizabeth on 15th November 1950 . . . A busy schedule had been arranged for the Princess's visit to Swindon in the Jubilee Year of the Borough, marking 50 years, almost to the day, since the incorporation of the two former urban districts of Old Swindon and Swindon New Town as the Borough of Swindon on November 9th 1900. To the delight of all, she managed to fit in a comprehensive Royal tour of the town, and cheering crowds gathered at various spots along the route to catch a glimpse of the Princess. However, there was a solemn note to her visit too, as her first stop after the ritual signing of the Visitors' Book at the Civic Offices was the Garden of Remembrance, where were assembled the relatives of men

and women of the Borough who had given their lives for their country between 1939 and 1945. The Princess inspected the Guard of Honour and went on to declare the Garden open; the opening ceremony was followed by a service of dedication, and Princess Elizabeth proceeded to Moredon Playing Fields, the next stage of her tour.

Inset: HRH The Princess Elizabeth's visit to Swindon on 15th November 1950 included a visit to BR (Western Region) Works, and she is seen here on the footplate of the Star class locomotive no 4057 The Princess Elizabeth. After a guided tour of the Railway Works, the Princess unveiled the name-plate of the newly-built locomotive no 7037. The last of the Castle class locomotives, it was named 'Swindon' in commemoration of the Jubilee of the Borough - a fitting

Events of the 1950s

WHAT'S ON?
Television hit Britain in a big way during the 1950s. Older readers will surely remember 'Double Your Money, Dixon of Dock Green and 'Dragnet' (whose characters' names were changed 'to protect the innocent'). Commercial television was introduced on 22nd September 1955, and Gibbs SR toothpaste were drawn out of the hat to become the first advert to be shown. Many believed adverts to be vulgar, however, and audiences were far less than had been hoped for.

GETTING AROUND
The year 1959 saw the development of the world's first practical air-cushion vehicle - better known to us as the hovercraft. The earliest model was only able to travel at slow speeds over very calm water and was unable to carry more than three passengers. The faster and smoother alternative to the sea ferry quickly caught on, and by the 1970s a 170-ton car-carrying hovercraft service had been introduced across the English Channel.

SPORTING CHANCE
The four-minute mile had remained the record since 1945, and had become regarded as virtually unbreakable. On 6th May 1954, however, Oxford University student Roger Bannister literally ran away with the record, accomplishing the seemingly impossible in three minutes 59.4 seconds. Bannister collapsed at the end of his last amazing lap, even temporarily losing his vision. By the end of the day, however, he had recovered sufficiently to celebrate his achievement in a London night club!

tribute to a Borough whose heritage was so closely linked with the growth of the railway. It was the railway works, opened more than a century previously, which had set Swindon on the road to prosperity, establishing Swindon New Town alongside the old market town and turning it into a thriving industrial centre. Sadly, the heyday of the Swindon Works as the home of the Great Western Railway was already, at the time of this photograph, in the past; nationalisation of the rail network had brought about the demise of the Great Western, along with all the other legendary railway companies whose passing is still mourned by steam enthusiasts everywhere. Swindon carried on making locomotives on a much smaller scale for British Railways until 1960, when Locomotive No 92220, the appropriately-named Evening Star, brought the era to an end, becoming not only the last steam locomotive to be built at Swindon but the last to be made for British Railways. With a grand total of 5,539 steam locomotives to its credit, the Works finally closed in 1986.

Shopping spree

Events of the 1960s

HOT OFF THE PRESS

Barbed wire, concrete blocks and a wide no-man's-land divided East from West when a reinforced wall was built right across the city of Berlin in 1961. Many East Germans escaped to the West at the eleventh hour, taking with them only the possessions they could carry. The Berlin Wall divided the city - and hundreds of family members and friends - for 28 years until the collapse of Communist rule across Eastern Europe. Who can ever forget those scenes in 1989, when ordinary people themselves began to physically tear down the hated wall?

THE WORLD AT LARGE

'One giant leap for mankind' was taken on 20th July 1969, when Neil Armstrong made history as the first man to set foot on the moon. During the mission he and fellow-astronaut 'Buzz' Aldrin collected rock and soil samples, conducted scientific experiments - and had a lot of fun jumping around in the one-sixth gravity. Twenty-one hours and thirty-seven minutes after their landing they took off again in their lunar module 'Eagle' to rejoin Apollo II which was orbiting above them, proudly leaving the American flag on the Moon's surface.

Cyclist a-plenty seem to have gone inside The Spot for bike bits on this fine bright day, if the array of bicycles neatly lined up along the kerb is anything to go by! The Spot was also a favourite place to buy sports equipment, with the tennis racket in the window suggesting that the photograph was taken in the summer months. The inter-war years had seen some scandalous developments in tennis clothing: in 1933 Bunny Austin, the British Davis Cup player, had cast off long trousers and appeared on Wimbledon's Centre Court in shorts - and the women were as bad, with top Spanish player Lilli de Alvarez wearing culottes in 1929 and

Billie Tapscott of South Africa coming on court wearing no stockings! However, one tradition at least was safe for the time being: tennis clothing remained all white. It is not only the athletic who are drawn to look in The Spot's windows, as the shop also sold games, and virtually everything for the keen modeller. Next door, Mac Fisheries - promoting Scotch kippers, cod fillets and lobster tails - had its origins in a project established by Lord Leverhulme in 1921 to help the impoverished Scottish crofters by turning them into fishermen, and to make the scheme work, he built up a chain of some 300 shops to sell their fish.

1968 *was a year of considerable unrest - student protests and the Black Power salute at the Olympic Games*

Above: We have put this photograph of the Market Bookstall under the microscope and deciphered a date of September 1968. This was a year of considerable unrest - student protests, the Black Power salute at the Olympic Games, and the cancellation of the MCC tour of South Africa because of South Africa's refusal to accept the inclusion of the legendary all-rounder Basil d'Oliveira in the English team. It was also a year of funerals: Martin Luther King, Robert Kennedy, Tony Hancock, Bud Flanagan and Enid Blyton. And it was a year when some of us swallowed hard and wondered what the world was coming to: we had to come to terms with the musical Hair, the art of Andy Warhol, and an apparently ever-widening gulf between the generations. Fred Trueman retired and the Chancellor slapped an extra 5d on a gallon of petrol and a packet of cigarettes. Better to escape inside the covers of Practical Householder, Motoring, Hi-Fi Sound, Football Weekly or Vanity Fair.

Below: Down came the rain - the little group standing in the doorway of Stead & Simpson's at 58a Bridge Street look as if they have just bought Wellingtons all round, and it is to be hoped that there are plenty more in stock alongside the sandals, winklepickers, court shoes, Louis heels, crepe soles and other 50s footwear. Remember those rubber galoshes that we used to pull on over our normal shoes to keep them dry? They worked well in moderately wet or snowy weather, but anything over ankle-deep came over the top - and this flood could have been well over ankle-deep in places. Wellingtons were what you needed. It seems that the Duke of Wellington believed in keeping his extremities dry; in addition to bequeathing his name to the Welly boot he was also an early patron of the umbrella, and

his patronage did much to enhance its popularity. Umbrellas were not considered modish until around 1800, but thereafter they became fashion accessories for gentlemen. Indeed, so indispensable were they that on one occasion - so the story goes - British officers, while under fire at Bayonne, put their umbrellas up to keep their uniforms dry. But a message came from the Duke of Wellington saying that he did 'not approve of the use of umbrellas during the enemy's firing and will not allow gentlemen's sons to make themselves ridiculous in the eyes of the army.'

Bottom: The rings with which many generations of Swindon couples plighted their troth came from this Regent Street shop; in the early years of the 20th

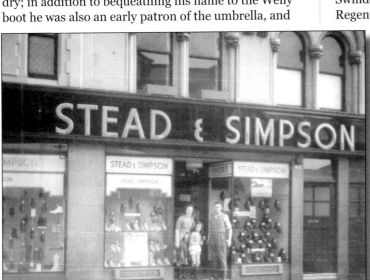

century it had been Cottell Brothers, also a jewellers, before becoming James Walker. This photograph is believed to date from 1945, so sales of wedding rings may well be just about to pick up significantly; many an engaged couple had decided to wait until after the war to tie the knot, making 1946 and 1947 boom years for weddings. Pursuing this line of thought leads one to reflect that the infant in the fine pram to the left of the picture is just a few years ahead of the post-war baby boom or 'bulge'. The sharp increase in the birth rate in Britain peaked around 1950. This in turn led to a significant expansion in the numbers recruited into teacher training establishments as the Government, which had set educational reform as one of its priorities, planned ahead to ensure a brighter future for the post-war generation.

Events of the 1960s

WHAT'S ON?

Television comedy came into its own in the 1960s, and many of the shows that were favourites then went on to become classics. 'On the Buses', 'Steptoe and Son', 'Till Death Us Do Part' and 'The Army Game' kept audiences laughing, while the incredible talents of Morecambe and Wise, the wit of Des O'Connor - often the butt of the duo's jokes - and the antics of Benny Hill established them for ever in the nation's affections. .

GETTING AROUND

The 2nd March 1969 was a landmark in the history of aviation. The Anglo-French supersonic airliner Concorde took off for the first time from Toulouse in France. Concorde, which can cruise at almost twice the speed of sound, was designed to fly from London to New York in an incredible three hours twenty minutes. The event took place just weeks after the Boeing 747, which can carry 500 passengers to Concorde's modest 100, made its first flight.

SPORTING CHANCE

Wembley Stadium saw scenes of jubilation when on 30th July 1966 England beat West Germany 4-2 in the World Cup. The match, played in a mixture of sunshine and showers, had been a nailbiting experience for players and spectators alike from the very beginning when Germany scored only thirteen minutes into the game. It was Geoff Hurst's two dramatic goals scored in extra time that secured the victory and lifted the cup for England - at last.

If you wanted to look smart for a job interview in 1945, Weaver to Wearer in Bridge Street was eager to kit you out for just thirty bob, leaving the Fifty Shilling Tailor at 90 Regent Street to eat his heart out! In fact, of course, both were excellent value. Next door, Keogh Bros is crammed full of household items - jugs, bowls, colanders and mats seem to be hanging up outside. Those setting up house in the postwar era had a much wider choice of kitchenware than their parents and grandparents had had - more and more items were

being made in plastic, while aluminiumware - prohibitively expensive when it was first made shortly before the first world war - had now come down in price, and many young housewives preferred it to the heavy iron and enamelware their mothers had invested in. Postwar homemakers also had the opportunity to take advantage of the development of the DIY trade - though to the less practically-minded, this was something of a mixed blessing - and it became possible for young couples to create a bright, modern, well-equipped home in which to start their happy married life. Just as long as they didn't hammer and drill too late at night and fall out with their new neighbours . . . Today, the aspiring homemaker might look for assistance of a somewhat different nature on this spot: it is now the Halifax Building Society.

When this photograph was taken, the cinema on the far right edge was still operating as the Arcadia. No doubt the name Arcadia was chosen because prior to the construction of the cinema, which opened in 1912, a small arcade of shops running back from Regent Street had occupied this spot. The shop at the left hand edge of the picture we believe to be Goddard & Co, Wine and Spirit Merchants, and next door to them Morse's department store appears to be displaying ladies' spring fashions. This successful Regent Street shop belonged to the Morse family, who started out as travelling salesmen, selling from door to door. Throughout the first half of the 20th century the family lived at The Croft; during their occupation the house became well-known locally for its beautiful flower displays. The Croft was built in

1840 and became the Morse family home in 1896. The head of the family at the turn of the 20th century, who rejoiced in the name of Levi Lappi Morse, and his son William Ewart Morse, both played distinguished roles in the community, serving as Mayor of Swindon and being elected MP for Wilton and Bridge-water, respectively. When William Ewart Morse died in 1952, the house and its grounds were sold for development, and became the Hesketh Crescent residential estate.

Events of the 1960s

MELODY MAKERS
The 1960s: those were the days when the talented blues guitarist Jimi Hendrix shot to rock stardom, a youthful Cliff Richard charmed the nation with his 'Congratulations' and Sandie Shaw won the Eurovision Song Contest for Britain with 'Puppet on a String'. It was the combined musical talents of a group of outrageous working-class Liverpool lads, however, who formed the Beatles and took the world by storm with music that ranged from the experimental to ballads such as 'Yesterday'.

INVENTION AND TECHNOLOGY
A major step forward was made in 1960 when the laser was invented. An acronym for Light Amplification by Stimulated Emission of Radiation, the device produces a narrow beam of light that can travel for vast distances and is focused to give enormous power. Laser beams, as well as being able to carry far more information than radio waves, can also be used for surgery, cutting, drilling, welding and scores of other operations.

SCIENCE AND DISCOVERY
When the drug Thalidomide was first developed during the 1950s it was hailed as a wonder drug which would ease the distressing symptoms of pregnancy sickness. By the early 1960s the drug's terrible side effects were being discovered, when more than 3000 babies had been born with severe birth defects. Malformed limbs, defective eyes and faulty intestines were the heart-rending legacy left by Thalidomide.

Above: September 1960 is the date given for this photograph; judging from the Post Office's open windows and the general absence of overcoats the weather seems to be mild, and the pavement in Regent Circus is crowded with shoppers. Beale's Snack Bar, a few doors along from F Maybury's, can expect to do a good trade in fizzy pop. The billboards on the right of the picture draw our attention to the Olympic Games; the 1960 Olympics, staged in Rome, ended on 12th September, and might be best remembered by many people as the first time they saw Muhammad Ali in action when, as Cassius Clay, he won the light-heavyweight boxing gold medal. Another success story of the 1960 Olympics which warmed our hearts was that of Wilma Rudolph, the courageous American sprinter who overcame a childhood fraught with illness - including polio, double pneumonia and scarlet fever - to fulfil her ambition of representing her country in the Olympics, and furthermore winning three gold medals. And those of us who secretly thought the Americans won more than was good for them might have taken a sly pleasure in seeing the Soviet team's tally of gold medals rise to 43 as compared to the USA's 34, and their overall medal count reach 103 to a mere 71 for the USA. It is perhaps better not to ask how many Britain got.

The inscription W W Hunter above the first-floor windows of Woodhouse & Son's is still there today on the premises which is now a branch of Dolcis. During World War II you would have obtained your ration books from this spot, when Hunter's became the Food Office.

The type of pram occupied by the youngster in the family procession crossing the road is a typical baby carriage of the 50s and 60s, and although today's buggies have the advantages of being light, adjustable and easy to fold up, prams such as these had their advantages too. Not only could you hang your shopping bag from the pram handle, but you could also stow your parcels in the foot end of the pram, and push baby and shopping along together with a minimum of effort. Going back still further, the prams of the 30s and 40s were deeper and were actually designed with an inbuilt storage compartment underneath the padded board that baby lay on - you took out baby, lifted up the board, and there you had a capacious compartment where you could put extra blankets, bottles, or your shopping!

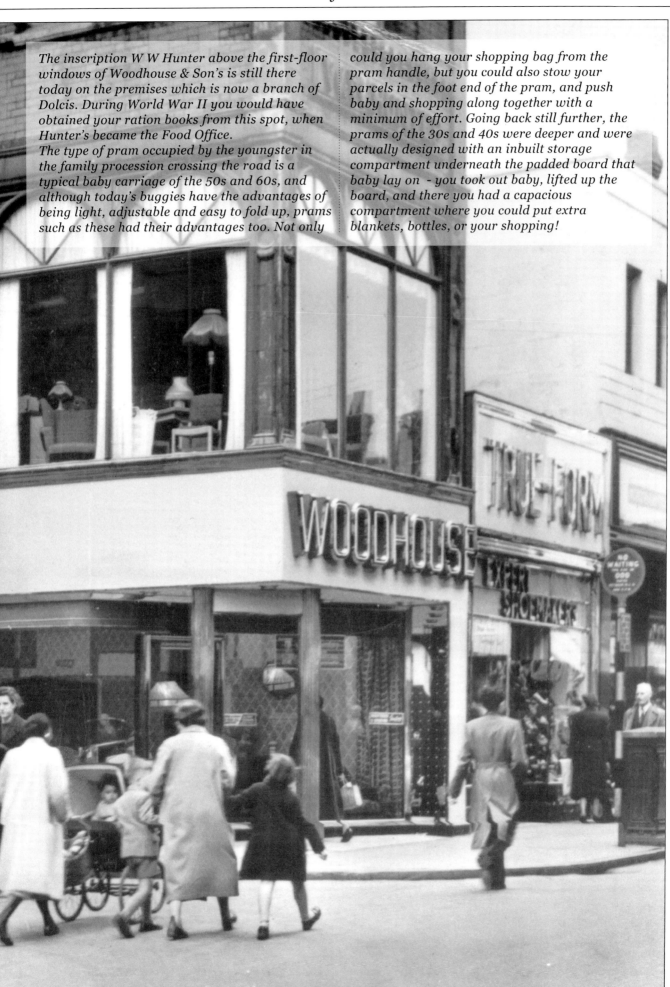

Bottom: As well as showing us places as they used to be, old photographs bring to mind the fashions and customs of times gone by. Here, for instance, we have an illustration of the rather more formal etiquette whereby a man would, as a matter of course, take the side of the pavement nearest the road when either walking beside a woman or passing her in the street. And they remind us of the tastes we have enjoyed through the years: on the hoarding to the left, two respectable men with the short back-and-sides of the day are inviting a glass of Mackeson to fulfil its promise, while visible to the rear of the Market Hall is the familiar hop leaf sign, the trademark of Simonds brewery. Simonds brewery, established in Reading in 1882 by the dynamic William Blackall Simonds, grew rapidly to become one of Berkshire's leading breweries, and its popularity then spread to the neighbouring counties. During the first half of the 20th century it was determined to prevent the London breweries from establishing themselves in the area, building up its holding of tied houses and taking over a large number of other brewers in the South and West of England. By the second world war Simonds was one of the area's leading brewers, with production running at some 279,000 barrels. After the war Simonds took over some more breweries and had a holding of over 1,200 licensed houses by the time it merged with the Courage group in 1960.

Right: Swindon's market moved to Commercial Road in 1892. For the 40 years or so prior to this, there had been an octagonal, partly-glazed covered market adjoining the Mechanics Institute, in the new town; one would have thought this would have been a good location for selling fish, meat, fruit and other goods to the rail workers, but for one reason or another it seems to have ended up in a rather run-down state, and the building was demolished in 1891 to make way for an extension to the Mechanics Institute. It was replaced by a new market composed of 17 shops and a triangular space for traders, built in Cromwell Street, down Commercial Road. The triangular area was originally open to the elements but was roofed over in 1903. The market continued in that form for more than 70 years, and many people will remember it looking pretty much as it does on this photograph dating from 1968. Harry Conn had this unit for many a year before it was taken over by Rebecca Conn in the late 60s. In 1977 the Market Hall was demolished and the site became a car park. It was then decided to build another market hall, and the somewhat futuristic white structure which houses the market today was opened in November 1994.

At work

This is what Whitehouse Road used to look like every day at the end of a shift at the Works. Looking at the men spilling out and making their way home, it is hard not to grow a little nostalgic for the steady routine of the working day before the workforce became more mobile and took to commuting and working flexible hours. Many of these men will have lived within walking distance of the Works; their families will have known almost to the minute when to expect them home, and their wives will have planned the meals accordingly. A job at the GWR Works was, up until the post-WW2 era, regarded as a job for life; and there were many openings for clerical staff as well as manual workers, with more than 1,500 people employed in the offices in 1926. And it was not only a job for life, it was also a job to be proud of - even if there were occasional grumbles over working conditions and management policies, the men (and women) enjoyed the respect of the whole nation, with the Swindon Works, along with the names of the many famous steam locomotives designed and built there, written indelibly into the history books.

Fish and chips, that great British institution, became popular during the 1920s

Proprietor Mr Todd, his daughter Florence Todd and an assistant pose for the camera inside Todd's, at No 77 Curtis Street, around 1923. Fish and chips, that Great British institution, became popular during the 1920s, and cost just a couple of coppers - tuppence, in other words. However, if coppers were a bit short, you could ask for a ha'porth of each and receive half quantity. Threepence has been rung up on the till, so either Todd's was more expensive than some, or the sale represents an extra portion. Of course, fish and chips used to feed the mind as well as the body -

traditionally, fish and chips always came wrapped in newspaper, and you could read yesterday's news as you ate. It didn't occur to us that eating newsprint might not be good for us, and when the Government decided that fish and chips must not come into contact with newspaper there was general indignation and everybody complained that the nation's favourite takeaway just didn't taste the same. But we kept eating it, and so after three-quarters of a century No 77 Curtis Street, though no longer Todd's, is still selling fish and chips.

Making and servicing the finest timepieces for over six generations

I n 1996 Deacon and Son (Swindon) Limited opened its new purpose built jewellery, clock and watch workshops, which are testament to the Company's experience and skill acquired over the last 150 years. Here, technicians repair and service all manner of clock, watch and jewellery repairs from antiques to the most modern design.

Deacons is an official Rolex retailer, a relationship that stretches back over three generations, and to this day Rolex remains Deacons' flagship watch brand.

Above: *The Regulator Clock, made by the company around 1865.*
Right: *The staff on the company's 100th birthday celebration outing to Bournemouth in 1948.*
Below: *The Wood Street premises in 1902.*

Since 1986, the company has had its own hallmark, registered at the Birmingham Assay Office. The jewellery workshop produces its own branded products including bangles, rings, earrings, pendants and cufflinks in silver, gold and platinum. As the New Millennium approaches the company is continuing to develop new products and ideas under the leadership of current Managing Director, Richard Deacon. Richard and sister, Sara - also a Director actively working in the business - are the sixth generation of the Deacon family to have been

CHINA **DEACONS** GIFTS

involved in the company. They continue to look to expand their individual and unique brand of customer service.

Deacon and Son (Swindon) Limited, was founded as a Jewellers, Watch and Clock makers by George Deacon in 1848. The catalyst for bringing the name of Deacon to Swindon was undoubtedly the arrival of the Great Western Railway. As an ambitious 26 year old George Deacon, having moved from his home town of Westbury, realised the need for time-keeping in a fast growing town of the industrial revolution. The business was able to expand, winning one of the timing contracts for the Great Western Railway on the line between Paddington and Swansea from the early 1850s until 1893.

It is difficult to imagine that in 1848 the California Gold Rush was yet to happen (1849) and Cecil Rhodes had not even contemplated opening up South Africa. In these

early days George Deacon was reliant on obtaining diamonds, precious and semi-precious stones from South America, in particular from Brazil where an agent was employed to bring back goods to England.

George was joined in the business by his nephews, Hubert and Joshua, with Hubert's entrepreneurial ability quickly becoming recognised. During the period of 1860 to 1890 the business expanded, producing a variety of time pieces, including long case clocks, trunk dial clocks, carriage clocks, pocket watches and even mercurial barometers. Some of the clock cases were even made from slate brought by rail from the quarries of South Wales. Many of these time pieces still exist to this day and are still serviced in the company's workshops. After succeeding his Uncle George, Hubert became the first President of the Swindon Chamber of Commerce in 1893 and was also responsible for supplying Swindon's first public clock on the Town Hall.

Hubert was also responsible for building a terrace of 122 houses, called Deacon Street, which remains to

Top: *The premises today.*
Above centre: *The jewellery workshop.*

including the Second World War, until he was joined by his son, Michael, in 1958.

Michael Deacon was another Hubert. Like his great grandfather before him, he had the drive, flair and vision to take Deacons' into an era of dramatic development from the moment he succeeded his father in 1970 until his death in 1998. He opened four branches in Highworth (1971), Wootton Bassett (1974), Faringdon (1976) and Tetbury (1981).

Michael was a clockaholic. He loved everything to do with the business and his enthusiasm rubbed off on all those around him. At the annual Christmas party, he used to say to each company member, "Are you a believer"? The true answer was that the staff believed in his ability. It was Michael who produced limited edition carriage clocks for the American market in the 1970s and was the inspiration behind the investment in the facilities at Wood Street. In the 1990s the old workshops were rebuilt and refurbished. The clock, jewellery and china departments were also overhauled. By 1998 his dream of a new super shop, fit for the 21st century, had been realised. That same year he celebrated the 150th anniversary of the founding of Deacon & Son. He died shortly afterwards, a man whose ambitions had been fulfilled.

Michael's widow, Joy, acts as a Company Director in charge of the China and Gift Shop. Richard and Sara Deacon will ensure that the company, one of few family run businesses to have spanned so many generations, continues the family legacy that Hubert, Jack and Michael, in particular have left.

Left: A carriage clock made by the company recently.
Below: Michael Henry Deacon (1935-1998).

this day. Hubert established a branch shop on Fleet Street that dealt exclusively in china and glassware.

Hubert's son, George, took over the running of Deacons in the early 1900s. A keen athlete George was Captain of Swindon Gym Club and was also a Sergeant in the Wiltshire Yeomanry. Unfortunately George contracted TB, a disease from which he died at the early age of 37 in 1913. His wife, Mildred (nee Pakeman), inherited the business in the most difficult of times. The Great War was only just over the horizon. During it, materials were in short supply and trade suffered. The shop on Fleet Street was sold. The depression years also meant that purse-strings were held tight and the company had to battle hard against the tide that washed many other businesses away. The running of Deacons' passed from Mildred to her eldest son HJ (Jack) Deacon. Her younger son, Guy, ran the china business. Jack was a successful businessman who steered the company through the difficult years

Foods to enjoy until the cows come home

Think of New Zealand, and you think of butter; think of Cornwall, and you think of cream. So if a Cornishman emigrates to New Zealand, you would expect him to become involved in dairy-related activities. And this is what happened when Cornish-born Henry Reynolds emigrated to New Zealand in the early 1880s.

Mr Reynolds took up dairy-farming in the Waikato area, and in 1886 he had the brilliant idea of building a butter-making factory at Pukekura, near Cambridge, NZ. We know that before this time a number of cheese factories had been adapted for buttermaking, but Henry Reynolds' factory is generally regarded as the first factory to be built specially for the purpose of making butter. The plant consisted of a steam-engine, a Burmeister & Wain separator, a churn and a butter-worker. Production duly commenced; and when the butter was ready, it needed a brand-name, so Mr Reynolds chose the name of 'Anchor'. It is said that he was looking around the factory for inspiration - and he espied a tattoo on the arm of one of his engineers! The anchor has long been associated with reliability and safe arrival. Samples of Anchor butter were sent to the 1888 Melbourne Exhibition. And it won first prize.

Right: *The transportation of butter churns.*
Below: *1920s advertising.*

However, Britain was not to have an opportunity to taste the prize-winning Anchor butter for almost 40 years. By this time the thriving business and the successful trademark upon which it was based were owned by the New Zealand Dairy Association. This organisation had been formed in 1888; the Reynolds family, having built up their business from one butter factory to eight, had sold to NZDA in 1896.

The Association subsequently became a Co-operative five years later.

New Zealand butter had made its first appearance in Britain in 1882, having embarked upon its journey across the world almost by chance. On February 15th of that year the sailing ship Dunedin, 1,200 tons, left Port Chalmers, New Zealand, bound for England. She had on board the first shipment of frozen meat; but the meat did not completely fill the refrigerated storage available, and so a small consignment of butter from the Edendale Dairy Factory was loaded just to fill the space. So after a passage of 98 days, on 24th May, the first New Zealand butter was

Above: A 1920s delivery van, complete with resplendent driver.
Top: The company's advertising can be seen on the wall of this house.

unloaded at London Docks, and was sold for elevenpence ha'penny a pound.

Britain then had to wait until the following year to taste New Zealand butter again. On this occasion seven kegs of butter were shipped across under refrigeration in the Lady Jocelyn.

It was not until the period between the wars that Anchor butter became an established part of the British diet. By 1918 the Dominion's dairy produce was no longer subject to the fixed price imposed by the British Government during the war years and speculative trading had once more begun to come to the fore, and during the 1920s and 30s Tooley Street was in effect the marketing centre for Empire dairy produce. This street runs parallel with the south side of the River Thames, between Tower Bridge and London Bridge; it was lined with warehouses, many of which are equipped for cold storage, abutting onto the wharves. Some 27 firms along Tooley Street used to handle butter and cheese imports from the Dominions. Hays Wharf, established in 1770 and the principal wharf on Tooley Street, then entered into negotiations with the New Zealand Dairy Produce Board, a body formed in the mid-1920s to look after the interests of the entire New Zealand dairy industry, and in 1928 a contract was agreed which made Hays Wharf responsible for all aspects of the dairy trade with New Zealand.

Meanwhile, NZDA had in 1919 amalgamated with its rival, the Waikato Dairy Company Limited, to form the New Zealand Co-operative Dairy Company Limited. NZDA had wisely retained the successful Anchor brand, and it was this which was adopted as the registered trademark of the newly-formed company. In the early 1920s NZDC began to

explore the potential of the British market, setting up a London office in 1922; and two years later the Anchor brand made its first British appearance as retail packet butter at the 1924 Empire Exhibition in Wembley, where it was sold in 1lb cartons - with a free Anchor butter knife. Three years later a factory was set up in Upper Thames Street to pack Anchor butter for the domestic market.

Over the next ten years Anchor - 'The Leading Brand of the Choicest Butter from the Loveliest Dairy Pastures in the World' - became a well-established and popular brand. In 1929 Anchor, together with a variety of other New Zealand and Australian goods such as salmon, tinned oysters, cheese, evapo-rated milk and Sunny South Australian butter, became the responsibility of Empire Dairies, a limited company formed from an amalgamation between NZCDC and the Australian Producers Wholesales Federation. Empire Dairies marketed Anchor with great success; their network grew to cover such towns and cities as Bristol, Cardiff, Birmingham, Manchester, Liverpool, Glasgow, Newcastle and Nottingham, and in 1934 it hit upon the idea of the 'Anchor Club'. Readers may remember collecting Anchor wrappers, to be exchanged for badges, and receiving birthday cards from Uncle Anchor; members also received a monthly

magazine. By the time the Anchor Brand reached its Golden Jubilee in 1936, the turnover of Empire Dairies had risen to £5,628,000, and with advertisements appearing in the newspapers, on posters and in shop windows, it was enjoying a high profile all over the country. This was further enhanced by its model cows which began to graze around various points of sale - forerunners of those irresistible dancing cows which made their first TV appearance in 1986, and the even more famous footballing cows which became essential viewing in 1988.

During the war years all butter and cheeses were requisitioned by the Government, and branding was discontinued - butter was butter, and you were lucky to get it! The low-quality margarine which was available as a substitute was universally disliked. Most families saved their butter ration for Dad's sandwiches, for guests or for a weekend treat. Many members of Empire Dairies' staff transferred to the Ministry; those who were called up were paid a retainer by the company, and virtually all those who returned from active

Above: 1940s advertising.
Top: Overseas exports.

service went back to their jobs after the war. Empire Dairies was contracted to supply the Royal Navy, and further contributed to the war effort by sending a cheque for £5,000 to the Minister of Aircraft Production for the purchase of a Spitfire, and another £5,000 to the Lord Mayor of London's fund for the relief of air raid victims.

In 1953, the year before butter rationing came to an end, Empire Dairies was sold to NZ Dairy Products Marketing Commission, and two years later a £12,000 advertising campaign announced the return to the shops of the Anchor brand. During the latter half of the 50s Anchor butter was promoted by a team of seven retail salesmen who toured the south of England in vans, canvassing the shops. Butter sales soared into the 60s as family finances were restored and families reacted against years of rationing, bringing up their children to enjoy butter, and while an increasing number of brands of butter came onto the market (in 1960 there were 150 New Zealand butter brands available in the UK) Anchor, with its newly-designed logo and packet, was

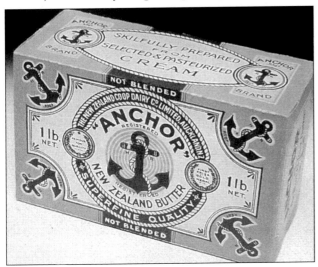

among the top sellers - and was the first butter to give a 'consumer guarantee' offering dissatisfied customers a replacement pack.

The next decade brought two significant changes to our shopping habits: the first was the introduction into Britain of the American-style Supermarkets, and the second was arrival of commercial television and the growing influence of television advertising on the nation's purchasing decisions. TV adverts were an effective means of encouraging consumers to try new products, and butter brands seized the new promotional opportunities. Anchor's first television advertisement was shown in 1962, and its advertising campaign was certainly effective as by 1965 sales of Anchor had reached 55,529 tons, half of which was packed by contract packers, and by 1969 Anchor, with record sales of 68,000 tons, was UK's best selling butter.

By 1969 another contemporary preoccupation had made an early appearance - healthy eating. Flora margarine was launched in 1967, and, by emphasising the fact that it was 'high in polyunsaturates' (a 'good thing' in those days), cleverly encouraged consumers to believe that in buying a cheaper and more spreadable product they were also looking after their family's health. This was the first serious attempt to change the nation's preference for butter; margarine's distasteful associations with the war years, rationing and a nasty taste had begun to fade with the passage of time, while the young housewives of the late 60s were from the post-war generation. So the margarine-or-butter question became a burning issue, with every housewife left to make her own decision according to her conscience. The differences in attitude between the generations became more marked; younger women became figure-conscious, dieting became

Left: *A 1920s butter packet.*
Below: *A window display from the 1930s.*

fashionable, and low-calorie and low-fat products began to proliferate; some youngsters were - much to their grand-mothers' disgust - raised on margarine. In the meanwhile Anchor had launched itself into cheese, with its half-pound retail packs of cheddar becoming available in 1972 and going on to become a brand leader.

It was in 1978 that plans were announced for the construction of a multi-million pound Anchor factory near Swindon, making this a very important year both for the future of Anchor butter and for the future of the town. Another significant event for Anchor was Empire Dairies' change of name, in August of that year, to Anchor Foods Limited. The new factory at Swindon was to provide Anchor Foods with a central point of supply for the whole of the country. This major investment on the part of its parent company, the NZ Dairy Board, demonstrated its long-term commitment to Anchor Foods and the UK market.

So in September 1979, on a muddy site right out at Blagrove, originally Blagrove Farm, with a view over fields and a few houses at Washpool, the first packets of butter were produced at Swindon in September 1979, although the official opening ceremony, performed by the Duke of Kent, did not take place until June 1980. Over the next six years or so the company built up its operations at Swindon; its original staff of 160, including a team of five telesales girls and a transport department with a fleet of 25 lorries - the first lorries the company had ever owned - was complemented in 1984 by a new four-strong marketing team, and the following year the factory expanded onto the neighbouring site which

Right: *A 1950s demonstration...*
Below: *...and a stall from the 1960s.*

was originally leased from Tempco and is still known as the Tempco site. By the time Anchor celebrated its Centenary in 1986, 325 people were employed at Swindon. Today, 20 years after production began, and with over 40 of the original workforce still working there and able to share many a curious reminiscence of the early days with newer colleagues, Anchor continues to provide valued employment opportunities for the local community.

The 80s were a period of product diversification for Anchor. Anchor Real Dairy Cream in a can, using fresh cream from local farms, was introduced in 1982, and meanwhile EEC

butter was packed and sold as Acorn butter, to differentiate it from straight New Zealand butter. 1983 saw the launch of mature and vintage cheddar, cheese and butter catering portions, followed by 'Shake' milk-shake drink, savoury butters and pot creams; by 1986 Anchor had a portfolio of some 50 products.

Throughout this period the question of Healthy Eating had continued to preoccupy the nation. Attitudes swung from one extreme to the other; at one point during the 80s many people were prepared to sacrifice Epicurean pleasure and buy whatever the latest 'scientific' evidence suggested was best for their health, so Anchor obligingly launched Half Fat Butter in packet form for those who no longer 'dared' to buy butter. More and more conflicting 'evidence' was brought to

light, however, and by the 90s most consumers had realised the futility of trying to avoid every food which had at one time or another been named as a 'health risk'. Many were only too glad to turn their back on the elusive concept of Healthy Eating and go back to the foods they enjoyed - including butter. In 1994 butter sales rose for the first time in many years.

Today the range of products includes Anchor Spreadable (launched in 1991) and Anchor SoSoft (a blend of Anchor Butter and vegetable oil) both aimed at today's families wanting the convenience of a spread with the taste of real butter. The Born Free campaign in 1997 was initiated to emphasise the fact that cows in New Zealand are outdoors all year round, in the sunshine, feeding on lush, natural pasture. These happy dairy herds, with their cute calves, effectively reminded customers that after all these years, Anchor Butter is still the best.

In July 1999 Anchor Foods Limited sold the assets and the business and changed its name to New Zealand Milk (UK) Limited, and Swindon began to get used to the distinctive yellow, green and blue New Zealand Milk logo, which symbolises warm sunshine, green pasture and the clear river running by - and also stands for vitality, taking the form of a leaping figure. However, we have been assured that the Anchor trademark - which this year celebrates the 75th anniversary of its first appearance at the Empire Exhibition at Wembley - will continue to appear as the sign of quality on our dairy products, and many of us will continue to think of our favourite butter as Anchor, for the rest of our lives!

Above: *The aerosol cream packing line in the mid 1990s.* ***Left:*** *Anchor Spreadable Butter being packed in tubs in the mid 1990s.*

Family friendly shopping that keeps getting better and better

Everyone in Swindon will agree that a trip to the Brunel Shopping Centre is a great way to spend a day. When they try to explain exactly what they love about it, however, their views may differ a little. For some, it's the choice of shops; you can wander round to your heart's content, and with stores such as House of Fraser, Marks & Spencer, Boots, C&A and Argos to choose from, you will never get bored. Others - the ones who go shopping with a more definite purpose in mind - will say that they always make a beeline for the Virgin Megastore, or Dillons, or one of the electronics shops such as Tiny Computers and Tandy, or their favourite out of the many quality fashion retailers, because they know they will find exactly what they want. For others still it's the safe, convenient parking and the comprehensive facilities which make going to the Brunel Shopping Centre such a pleasant and hassle-free experience; while for many people a day out isn't complete without a snack or two, so they will mention McDonalds and the various other restaurants and coffee bars. And anyone below waist height will probably tell you the best thing of all is the Brunel Tots Soft Play Centre, with its slides and climbing stairs and soft toys.

But while younger generations of Swindon shoppers have grown up safe in the knowledge that there's something for everyone at the Brunel Shopping Centre, their parents and grandparents will still remember how

Right: *The Brunel Shopping Centre.*

different town centre shopping was in the 50s and 60s. By the late 60s change was definitely in the air; the post-war decline of the railway industry had brought pressure upon Swindon Council to make the town more attractive to new industry, and the Council had been quick to respond by embarking on a programme of urban development. Up to the second world war Swindon had been a one-street town whose facilities, whilst adequate to accommodate the basic needs of its resident population,

the Brunel Shopping Centre began.

With the needs of the shopper in mind, the Council decided that the new centre should provide protection from the elements; also, all shop frontage should be continuous and easy for pedestrians to negotiate. After much careful planning and designing, the first phase of the building work finally began on 17th December 1970, operating to a construction sequence which had been so designed that as many of the existing shops as possible could continue trading for as long as possible. Sainsburys was the first store to be completed and opened, and immediately became a magnet for customers; the destruction and rebuilding of Regent Street was left until the end of this phase of construction and was not carried out until 1975. The first phase of new shopping centre - the large rectangular Plaza building, surrounded by transparent canopy and a stainless steel fascia - was well received by shoppers and critics of architecture alike; subsequent phases included the Plaza itself, Canal Walk, Havelock Square, the car park, the Arcade and the David Murray John building. One leading architect commented that 'This all works admirably, in itself, and in relation to the surrounding town', and comparisons were frequently drawn between Swindon's new Brunel Shopping Centre and the renowned Galleria in Milan.

By the end of the decade the project, costing some £30 million in total, was complete, providing Swindon not only with around 50,000 square metres of additional retail space but also with new offices, residential accommodation and public areas. Throughout the development, great care had been taken to combine impressive design features with functionality, and the Centre was highly effective in

did not reflect the modern trends in retail development. The Council recognised that the town would only expand and prosper if they could transform it into a place where people wanted to live and work; and in order to do that, major investment was necessary. So they began planning for the future, with radical projects which included the construction of the inner ring road, car parks, and better shopping facilities.

The first improvement from the shopper's point of view was the development of The Parade, which added another street to the town centre shopping area. This, however, was just the beginning; the Council's regeneration schemes were proving successful and the population was growing rapidly, and by the 60s it was clear that further shopping provision was necessary. It was decided that the opposite side of Regent Street should be developed into a large shopping centre; and so the concept of

Top left: *The bright, relaxed atmosphere of the 'new' Brunel Shopping Centre.* ***Above:*** *The Brunel Plaza with its distinctive new atrium.*

meeting the various needs of all sectors of the growing community in a modern and appealing way. The David Murray John Tower, a 20-storey high-rise block, comprised ten floors of offices with ten floors of residential flats above. Visually, the centre of Swindon was greatly enhanced by the pedestrianised area with its canopies, the arcaded entrances and the walkways, while inside the air-conditioned Mall a 'travelator', as the moving walkway was termed, contributed to the overall impression of movement and bustle as it took shoppers from level of shops to another. There was a covered market; there was even a ballroom; and the very fine Plaza was an ideal setting for Salvation Army recitals and children's entertainments, especially at Christmas and other festive occasions - no doubt some readers will remember begging and pleading for another ride on the carousel in the Plaza, in the midst of the hustle and bustle of the Christmas shopping. The Council's investment paid off; by the late 70s Swindon, with its expanding population and its thriving and diverse industrial base had become one of the busiest and most successful commercial centres in southern England.

Right: *The original Marks and Spencer building on Regent Street incorporated into the Centre.*
Below: *Brunel Shopping Centre seen from Market Street.*

specific structural alterations and relocations. First of all, it was decided that the Indoor Market would benefit from being moved to a fresh location outside the Arcade; its place would then be taken by a House of Fraser department store, which it was felt would be more in keeping with the nature of the surrounding retail outlets. Then, a new Mall was to be introduced at first floor level in the Plaza, to allow more shops to establish a presence inside The Centre and increase the customer's choice. Finally, to complement the increased the level of activity on the first floor, it was planned to construct a connecting bridge between the Arcade and the Plaza at first floor level to allow shoppers to circulate more freely.

Over the next 20 years the growth of the town continued, and as the area's economy developed, so the profile of its population gradually changed. The manufacturing industries which represented Swindon's traditional heritage were disappearing and were being replaced by new service-based employers, and this shift in emphasis was reflected in the lifestyle of the town's new residents. In 1994 it was decided that the time was right to implement a major refurbishment project to bring the Brunel Centre into line with Swindon's new expectations. Refurbishment plans were drawn up, outlining what was needed to achieve maximum impact. Broadly speaking, the objective which the management set itself was to improve the overall ambience and shopping experience of The Centre, and the means of achieving this was by giving all public areas a bright, fresh, modern image, introducing modern customer service facilities and making a number of

The first phase of the refurbishment commenced in early 1995, and the project was completed during the autumn of 1997 - and, as during the initial construction of the Centre, disruption for retailers and their customers was kept to an absolute minimum while building works were in progress. Swindon's shoppers were delighted by the results. With an undercover shopping area containing more than 70 stores, the Brunel Shopping Centre now offers visitors an exciting and satisfying shopping experience, seven days a week. There are top fashion stores such as New Look and Burtons; there are household stores such as Whittards of Chelsea, Cargo Homeshop and Houseworks; there are sports shops, toy shops, jewellers, stationers, opticians, travel agents, a hairdressers, charity shops - in fact,

Both pictures: *The Brunel Arcade today.*

there is everything you could possibly need; and just in case you can't immediately find what you are looking for, a team of friendly Customer Assistants are there to help. Those with limited mobility will find access easy, with automatic doors into all shopping areas, lifts in the Arcade and the Plaza, disabled toilets and dedicated parking spaces in The Brunel North Car Park, which gives direct access onto Level 3 of the Centre. This car park has in fact won The Secured Car Park Award for its safe parking, ease of access and customer service facilities which include 'pay on foot' machines and change machines; the Centre believes that parking, like everything else, should be made as easy and as customer friendly as possible.

In line with this belief it has implemented a no smoking policy to ensure that the atmosphere is as pleasant as possible for all visitors; it provides pleasant Parents Rooms to ensure a congenial and hygienic environment for changing nappies and feeding; and it also sponsors the Safe Child Scheme, which means that wristbands are available and all its staff are trained to deal with lost children as quickly

*Top:Children enjoying Christmas celebrations in the Brunel Shopping Centre. **Left:** The Bridge Link. **Above:** The Arcade.*

and safely as possible to reunite them with their parents. In short, the Centre has done everything it can think of to make shopping safe and enjoyable; but the Management Team is always eager to receive feedback from customers, and any comments and suggestions for new ways to improve any aspect of shopping at the Brunel Centre are welcomed.

It is this pro-active and positive attitude which has kept the Brunel Centre as popular as ever through the many changes of the last 30 years. When the Centre was begun in 1970, nobody could have been

sure what it would look like by the end of the century, or how shopping trends would change. Looking back over that period now we can appreciate what an important part the Brunel Shopping Centre has played in those changes, simply by maintaining its original policy of providing the very best in shopping, with that little bit extra - extra entertainment for the kids, extra convenience for the grown-ups, and extra shops for everyone. MEPC, the international property company who acquired the Brunel Shopping Centre in July 1999, has affirmed its commitment to further improving the shopping experience in the Brunel Shopping Centre and Swindon Town Centre, and so, although we may not know exactly what exciting developments the future will bring, we do know that we can look forward to the prospect of many, many more great days out in the Brunel Shopping Centre.

Left: The Arcade following completion of the refurbishment programme.
Below and bottom: *The Brunel Plaza today.*

The crowning glory of the dental industry

Associated Dental Products (ADP) Ltd has a proud place in the pecking order of Swindon's commercial sector. Since 1941 it has been based at its Kemdent Works' site in Purton. It is one of the few dental companies that are manufacturing in this country. Even the other main competitors are from overseas - USA, Japan and Germany. ADP stands out as one of the major UK player on this field. Mention dental products to the man in the street and he will immediately come up with the cartoon stereotype of granny's teeth in a glass. Failing that, he will come up with the oldie about then dentist telling you that your teeth are OK, but your gums will have to come out. If he stopped to think, he would realise that the world of dental care and accessories is far greater than he had at first thought. It has come a long way from the false teeth made from wood that the first American president, George Washington, was reputed to have sported. We are now into a realm of scientific research and state of the art technology. As the

world markets have become more sophisticated, so have the products. The company makes polishing wheels that can deal with precious metals as well as natural teeth. There are polyester foil strips, filling materials and zinc oxide cements, waxes for bite registrations, tooth stain removers, mouth washes, knives, mixers and ointments. Oh yes, there are also denture materials.

Right: *White overalled girls at work in the wax processing and packing department.*
Below: *Working in the laboratory in the early 1950s.*

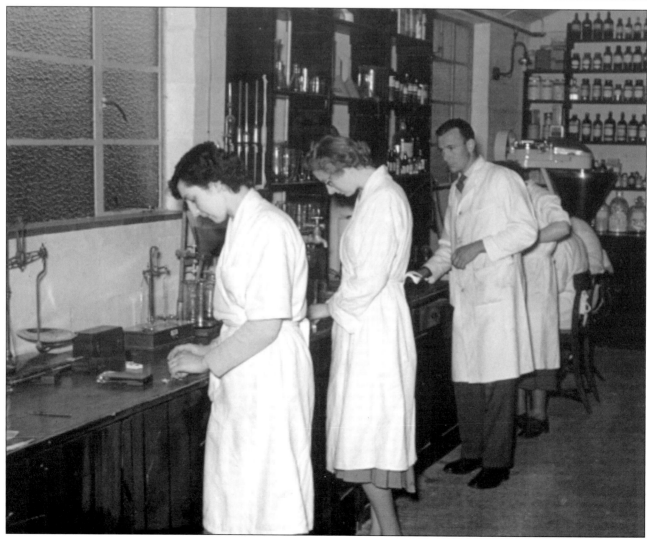

Kemdent is the registered trademark of the company that was set up in 1922 in London's West Ealing. Harold Osborn was the company founder. He had worked for Western Dental, selling their dental products, when he decided that, instead of working to make someone else comfortable, he could do that for himself. He

arranged financial backing with two dentists who saw that there was an opening in the market that Osborn could fill. He set about acquiring a number of small dental manufacturing units in order to make a range of dental products. These were then sold to the dental distributors who would arrange for the retailing of these to individual dentists and surgeries. It was not until 1997 that the company targeted dentists directly. Now direct selling takes place and plans are afoot to increase this sales approach. The scope is there. There must be something like 20,000 dentists in the UK. The dental dealers still sell many of the company products on its behalf, but direct selling is

an approach that may well be developing rapidly in the 21st century.

A new range of dental wax products was brought to the company in 1928 when Mr & Mrs Amos J Cakebread joined from the Esher Manufacturing Co Ltd. Amos

worked for the company for 40 years. In those years the basic range of products was largely unchanged. Some of those produced before the war are no longer in existence, but the staple diet of wax products continued to form the hub of the business. It was the process of manufacture of those products, particularly the modelling wax that has been the top line, that was to change dramatically. Once, the hot, molten wax was poured into large tin trays and left to set. It was then taken out of the

Top: *The London Dental Trade Exhibition in May 1936.*
Above: *The British Dental Exhibition - London 1954.*

trays and guillotined into thin sheets. Wax could be toughened by rolling thinner blocks into sheets. These blocks were made by pouring a scoop of hot molten wax from the melting coppers into the setting trays. There were hundreds of them. The girls employed to do this must have been shattered by the end of the day. Once cooled, the trays were taken into another room for separation and the empty trays sent back to the racks. Guess what? Then the process started all over again! Nowadays, a specialised conveyor system, with little manual effort, carries out this task. Powered trimmers have taken over the task of cutting the sheets to size.

The early 1940s was a time when Londoners anxiously watched the night skies. The bombers of Goering's Luftwaffe paid frequent visits to the capital. Homes and businesses were obliterated as that hail of death fell from the skies above. Kemdent was not to be spared. It re-located to Purton in 1941. The premises that it took over had been a jam factory and then a dairy at different times in its history. However, there was not too much in the way of jam or cream in the commercial world during the Second World War. Materials were in short supply as everything was channelled towards the war effort. Building expansion was equally difficult. All manner of different construction materials had to be used in a mend or make do sort of fashion. There were wooden huts mixing with Nissen huts and those made from concrete blocks. Eventually, these were joined together by covered passages in one giant jigsaw. Mr Osborn helped Kemdent play a part in the war effort. He collaborated with the inventor of the jet engine, Sir Frank Whittle, in researching the 'lost wax' process for precision casting in the mass production of the jet engine. Another effect of aviation on the company was in the development of a new type of cavity lining cement to be used underneath fillings. Pilots of high altitude planes had complained of toothache. It was discovered that the problem was to be found in the inadequate protective insulation underneath a tooth filling. Fans of Trivial Pursuits can now answer the question about the link between jet aircraft and the dental industry!

After the war, Associated Dental Products Ltd, as it had now become, continued to establish a solid and

Above: *The new offices opened December 18th 1998.*
Top: *The premises in the 1950s.*

expanding client base for its business. The birth of the NHS saw a large demand for the company's products, though this levelled off after a while. The 1956 Suez crisis threw the world into a panic as it was feared that the loss of oil supplies and price increases would cause supply problems for the dental wax industry. A year's worth of orders was taken in four months. Amos Cakebread's son, Donald, took over as Works Manager in 1968 when his father retired. This coincided with the start of a period of further growth for ADP. A wholesale dental company, Percy J Clark & Co Ltd (PJC), had been operating as ADP's export agent for over 30 years. Before the war, Percy had travelled the world looking for dental products for his company and for customers for ADP. Associated Dental bought out PJC in 1968 and, four years later, Donald Cakebread became the parent company's joint Managing Director with Gerald Hatton, Percy Clark's nephew.

In 1977, another subsidiary was acquired. Precious Metal Techniques, with the unfortunate abbreviation of PMT, had operated in London, specialising in the supply of 'Crown & Bridge' products. With the acquisition of PMT, along came the agency for supplying the dental products and precision attachments for Cendrex Metaux (Switzerland). This subsidiary was sold in 1994. In 1991, the company bought the business of the sale and distribution of

the Austenal range from Noblepharma UK Ltd. New buildings were built to help modernise the site, though a fire in 1993 slowed production for a while.

Gerald Hatton retired in 1986 and Donald Cakebread took over the company. Both is daughters, Sandra Cakebread and Wendy Mead, came to work for ADP, so creating a third generation of family involvement. Sandra became the Marketing Director and Wendy the Works Director. Together with fellow Directors, Peter Kirkby and Gary Squires they intend to further the company's reputation for quality by developing its waxes and filling materials to suit the demands of an ever more sophisticated market. There is a uniqueness about the manufacturing method and formulation that makes the modelling waxes special. They are used across the world by technicians who mould a trial denture that the dentist uses to check the fit. There are large markets for ADP's goods in Italy, Korea, France and South Africa. The markets are not confined to dentists, as jewellers and chiropodists are also customers. One product that is immensely successful is Diamond. This is a tooth-coloured filling material that sets quickly and is resistant to saliva. Because it is tasteless, it is very popular with children. You could say that Diamond is the jewel in ADP's crown.

Below: *The premises in 1998.*

Working for one of the best

Big is not necessarily beautiful. On the other hand, it would be foolish to think that every large commercial enterprise lacks the personal and considerate touch. Raychem is a company that is global in its dealings. So, in which caring category does it fall? The answer can be found in discovering that it features in the Collins publication '100 Best Companies to work for in Britain'. Not only is the reputation in Swindon high, but ranking among the best in the land marks Raychem as an employer that values its workforce as the life blood of its empire. That same consideration is given to providing a product of value that is creative and innovative. The focus is upon the requirements of the customer and the relationships developed have helped found a confidence and trust from the clients in what it is Raychem provides. As it continues to set itself stretching goals to be achieved, the company continues to deliver great results that keep shareholders, employees and customers satisfied. Even so, a good company does not sit on its laurels. Raychem is keen to keep on growing, setting itself an annual growth figure of 15 per cent.

The man in the street may not be familiar with the company name. He is probably not aware that he may be using Raychem's products on a daily basis. As a company that uses a wide range of diverse materials in developing thousands of products, there is an effect on the daily lives of millions of people across the world. Whenever a jumbo jet takes off, the electrical signals to the flight deck are carried by Raychem components. The

wiring and connectors that determine the pilot's flight path and the navigator's calculations all come from the laboratories and workshops of this multi-national. If you are cold, there is no need to reach for the control switch. In your home or at the factory, the Raychem self-regulating heater cables prevent pipes freezing and bursting with nasty claims whizzing off to the insurance company. There are circuit protection devices that help cars and computers perform reliably when they are turned on or booted up. Raychem produces wire,

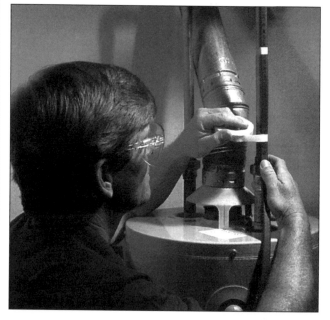

splicing and insulation parts that work away in the background whenever the phone rings or the lights are switched on. Thanks to the developments the company has made in its technology, based on the special properties of polymers, metals and chemicals, it has gained an international presence in the world of materials science.

The Raychem name may not be on the lips of the man in the street, but it is at his fingertips during a normal day in his life, whether he realises it or not.

Above: *Raychem engineers installing polymeric insulators.* ***Top:*** *Raychem Factory B - Cheney Manor.*

Life began for the company with the ideas of a chemical engineer from the East Coast of America. In the early 1950s, Paul Cook moved cross-country to the San Francisco Bay area. While everybody else seemed to be wrapped up in surfing and partying on the beach in the post-war euphoria that affected so many in the States, Cook turned his attention to more important matters. He went to work at the Stanford Research Institute. Here he saw the potential for a new branch of materials science. He focused on radiation chemistry. He studied and researched the use of high energy electrons to change the molecular structure of polymers. This was a time when the word 'radiation' struck fear into the hearts of the population. Everybody was familiar with the effects upon the people of the cities of Nagasaki and Hiroshima in 1945. To the general public, radiation was a killer sickness that knew few boundaries. It could eat into the flesh and cause painful death in a very short time. There were even rumours that unborn children could be affected. The media and the military did not help much. Army and air force generals regarded radiation as part of their armoury of defence against the threat of communism. Their only view of radiation was in relation to nuclear physics. Paul Cook took a purer view of the word. His focus was on the properties of heat transfer. He went to work to illustrate the positive and peaceful applications of his work.

Paul Cook set up the Raychem Corporation in Menlo Park, California in 1957. His first products were light-weight, but strong, wiring and cabling for the aircraft industry. Shortly afterwards, he produced heat-shrinkable tubing. His products had been developed from the research in radiation chemistry that enabled him to cross-link molecular chains. This made the material stronger and longer lasting. It could put up

with temperature swings and resisted abrasions. One other important feature that he discovered was that crosslinked polymers do not melt when they are heated. They just soften. This knowledge helped Cook develop the heat recoverable plastics technology in which Raychem pioneered and led the field. On a practical basis, this was translated into the production of sealing splices in electrical wiring harnesses and protective coatings on metal brake-line tubing.

Within three years, Raychem had become so successful that the company opened up in Europe. It was a wise move. This region was to become the most profitable of the company' global operations. By the late 1990s, 43 per cent of the annual turnover was generated here. Some 3,300 of Raychem's 8,000 employees earn their living in Europe. Its first foothold on this continent was in Braintree, Essex. There it stayed for six years until 1966. It was in World Cup year that the connection with Swindon was first made. A site was established at Cheney Manor. By 1969 a second factory had been set up there. They were simply known as factories A and B. As the work rolled in and the European markets grew, 34 acres were acquired at Dorcan to enable even more expansion. Two sites were developed at Dorcan, Site A and Site H. Site H is

Raychem's UK headquarters. All along, Swindon's municipal leaders were supportive of a company that brought jobs and prosperity to this part of Wiltshire. Large involvement in other industries such as aerospace, consumer electronics, automotive, marine,

Above: Raychem's founder, Paul Cook.
Top: Bob Reid head of Corporate Technology receiving the Queens Award for Technological Achievement from the Lord Lieutenant for Wiltshire, Field Marshal Sir Roland Gibbs.

telecommunications and railways has seen the order books full and the employees happy. Major contracts with British Telecom, the former energy utilities and the Ministry of Defence has seen Raychem heavily involved in the nation's developments in technology. The company's European Electronics OEM Division is based in Swindon. Here the manufacture of high performance wire and cable takes place. Heat-shrinkable tubing, markers and moulded parts are also in production. There is a sales support team for the telecommunications and utilities businesses. When Raychem first came to these shores, it had 20 people on its payroll. Within 40 years that number had increased to over 1,100.

Although Swindon is only part of a European operation that takes in all the major countries, with a Cypriot base that deals with the Middle East and Africa, the work done in the UK has gained official recognition. In 1972, Raychem won the Queen's Award for technology. The honour was bestowed upon the company because of its work in developing high voltage electrical terminations. The work done in producing Rayfort, a woven material that is used in telecommunication cable jointing, was recognised with another Queen's Award for technological achievement in 1993. This material had been developed at Swindon's European Corporate Technology laboratories. It more than met the needs of the network installers working on pressurised high volume telecom lines. Further work that came to the particular notice of the industry was that undertaken on Raychem's conventional heat closure system. In 1980 work was started to enhance its performance. The success of this can be demonstrated in the results that were achieved. The installation time for cable joints was cut from four hours to a mere 30 minutes per joint.

Already a world leader in heat-shrink tubing and touchscreens, Raychem now heads the field in the production of its low fire-hazard cable and polymeric circuit protection. As the Chief Executive has been heard to remark, Raychem is pursuing an exciting and challenging business strategy that is reliant on invention and new ideas. Happily, the workforce shares that view and is more than content to work for a company ranked as one of the best.

Left: *Arthur Thompson (left), Raychem's first MD handing over on his retirement to his successor, Brian Parker.*
Bottom: *Raychem's UK headquarters in Swindon.*

Solutions for those taxing problems

In the 1960s the Kinks sang, 'The taxman's taken all my dough' in one of their many hit records. It was something we could all relate to. Not only does taxation affect us all, but we share a common belief that the taxman is out to do us. Sometimes, it is our own fault. There are concessions and ways of cushioning the blow of the tax demand if only we could find them. Too often people plough their own furrow and fail to gain from the professional help that is available. They would not dream of pulling their own teeth or resetting their own broken legs. Yet, how many involve an accountant in their affairs? Even when PAYE is the norm, there is inheritance tax to be paid on the estate of a relative who has just died. There is self assessment for an increasing number of us. Many more people now have stocks and shares than ever before, especially since a number of building societies became banks. This ownership may make them liable for capital gains tax when the holdings are sold. How can the shopkeeper or one-man business hope to have either the time or the experience to be able to produce accounts that take into consideration all the tax relief entitlement and, at the same time, satisfy the Inland Revenue? The answer is simple. Consult the

Right and below: *Newport Street, the Company moved to the building with the blind in the 1960s.*

professional. The accountant is not in business just to serve the large company employer, but to offer the best practical advice and quality service to any client, whatever the size of turnover. The accountancy fees will be worth it, in giving peace of mind, cutting out wasted time and saving money. One of the top firms of chartered accountants in Swindon is Monahans Ledbury Martin.

The 15 partners and over 120 staff deal with in excess of 4,000 clients. With that level of experience and depth of expertise, it is unlikely that any problem you have has not been dealt with before.

There are now four offices operating under the banner of Monahans Ledbury Martin situated in Swindon, Trowbridge, Glastonbury and Chippenham. They are all linked with the latest high-tech equipment. Networked computers mean that an employee in one office can get to exactly the same information from the central database as another. They are connected to the internet and can surf the world for information. Facts and figures are stored on CD ROMs and specialised software produces business accounts and tax returns. There are fax machines, laser printers and photocopiers everywhere. How this would have seemed like a whole new world to Brian Monahan when he founded the firm in 1934. His sophisticated equipment

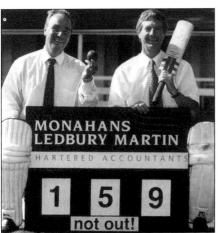

amounted to pens, paper and just a single typewriter. What he had in abundance was ability and a sense of purpose to succeed in the accountancy business. The heights of his achievements

can be measured in the distance the firm has travelled from those first days in a little lean-to office on Cricklade Street. There, sandwiched between the Goddard Arms Hotel and a solicitor's office, Brian took on his first handful of clients. It took time to build up a large client base. Brian's first clerk was Harold Gibbs. Sometimes, in those first days together, business was so slack that they would pass the time playing noughts and crosses. Before long, the noughts had become zeros on the end of pounds as business picked up. Harold was trained in accountancy by his boss and such was his loyalty to the firm that he spent his whole working life at Monahans, retiring after almost 50 years' service.

Top: *The new premises which were constructed on the Newport Street site in 1988.* **Above:** *Brian Monahan, far right, pictured with his family.*
Left: *Monahans and Ledbury Martin join forces in 1996, combining 159 years of service.*

As the business expanded partners were taken on board. Philip Pitt joined during World War II and Frank Boydell was brought into the fold in 1947, after his demob from the Royal Navy. Other partners who joined in the first years after the war included Gordon Kingsmill and Bill Dawe. They came in 1951 and 1953 respectively. The lean-to had long been left behind. After Monahans moved to offices opposite the Town Hall in Regent Circus, its first home became a ladies' hairdresser. It was later to be demolished. The firm continued to go from strength to strength. By the mid 1960s it was decided to expand further by demolishing the Regent Circus property and build a new office block on the site. Business was moved to temporary accommodation on Newport Street whilst the rebuilding was to have taken place. However, plans were changed. Monahans stayed at Newport Street and added a second property alongside the first building. A sign that things were really going well was the number of branch offices that Brian Monahan and his partners were able to open. At one time there were

five of these at Cirencester, Pewsey, Abingdon, Malmesbury and Chippenham. The firm had certainly moved on from the few hundred pounds it had earned in fees back in 1934. There are still some clients from those times who stayed with Monahans through the intervening years and are now served by the Monahans Ledbury Martin firm. This came into being in 1996 when Monahans merged with another long established Trowbridge firm. As well as serving clients and working in a professional field, a number of the partners and staff have happily given their time in public service as well as in support of their profession. Brian Monahan sat as a magistrate on the Swindon bench for many years. He rose to become Chairman before reaching the compulsory retiring age of 70. David Holder, who became the Managing

Top: *The company's premises at night.* ***Above:*** *Today's partners and staff at the Swindon office.* ***Left:*** *Tony Cohen, tax partner, advising a client.*

Partner in 1996, also gave service as a magistrate, becoming a JP in 1984. Philip Pitt was a former president of the West of England Society of Chartered Accountants Committee. Gordon Kingsmill was another to be the WESCA president, holding office in 1975/6.

As a major player in Swindon's financial services sector, Monahans Ledbury Martin has an annual turnover of around £4M. Since the merger, it has sought to develop its specialist services. It now owns two companies. One delivers computer services and the other financial services. The former service is a new direction for the firm. This company arm is called Chek-Tek and provides IT solutions for businesses of all shapes and sizes. Sometimes businesses need on site training and this is tailored to meet the particular needs of the company and its personnel. One particular example of the firm's ability to meet the requirements of the locality is the special service it gives to farmers. The farming unit is staffed by people who have relevant experience and offers cost effective production of farm accounts. Specialists in the tax department offer help in planning and compliance work. There are computer based tax systems and the availability of help in self assessment returns, agreement of liabilities and in dealing with the dreaded VAT man. Services offered to private clients help them manage their income tax returns and plan ahead to avoid taxes swallowing up money and possessions that a person wants to pass on to a loved one after death. Help with National Insurance problems and sheltering funds in tax free holdings like PEPs, ISAs and TESSAs are at the heart of the personal tax services on offer. Larger clients benefit

from the fast and efficient service given by the payroll administration package that Monahans Ledbury Martin provides. The corporate finance section helps with business planning and financial projections. It is also one of only two local firms with an insolvency department.

Most of the clients are businesses in Wiltshire and Somerset. A large number of Swindon businesses rely on the firm for advice and help. Those in Swindon range from small shops to companies with a turnover of upwards of £30M. They benefit from the full range of financial services on offer. The firm prides itself on offering a quality service at all times, given in a cheerful, friendly and professional way. It also gives advice in language that can be understood, rather than full of jargon and an attempt to blind with science. For example, one advisory pamphlet suggested the following health check for certain businesses: record every transaction, bank all takings, pay expenses by cheque, obtain tax invoices and do not employ casual labour without following pay regulations. Simple, easy to understand advice that is full of common sense based upon years of profes-sional experience. Having been here for as long as it has, Monahans Ledbury Martin aims to continue to be a leading firm in Swindon for just as long again.

Below: John Garrett celebrates the firm's 60th Anniversary in 1994, with former partners John Faulkner and Gordon Kingsmill and Ann Monahan, wife of the founder.

Tracking down Swindon's most successful site

A new concept in shopping was created in Swindon when the McArthurGlen Designer Outlet Great Western opened in March 1997. Here, right in the heart of the town, top manufacturers including Austin Reed, Aquascutum, Benetton, Burberrys, Jaeger, French Connection and Timberland offer a varied range of stock to the public at attractively-discounted prices, in the unique surroundings of the sympathetically-refurbished, 150-year-old Grade II listed buildings of the former Great Western Railworks, the industrial legacy of the great Isambard Kingdom Brunel. Each year many millions of visitors come from the near and far to spend a delightful day in this unique shopping centre where, surrounded by mementoes of Swindon's great past, they can browse to their hearts' content and go home with an exciting selection of designer bargains!

The creation of this new Designer Outlet Centre by McArthurGlen, which at a cost of some £40 million represents the UK's largest retail regeneration project, is the latest development in the growth of a town whose history is in itself a remarkable success story. Originally a small market town, Swindon became the home of the engineering works of the Great Western Railway in the mid-1800s and enjoyed

great prosperity during the railway's heyday. When the engineering works grew obsolete more than 100 years later, the town successfully re-created itself as an important centre for manufacturing, distribution, technology and corporate headquarters. So, having grown from small market town to major heavy engineering base in the 1880s, Swindon then evolved

Above: The Great Western Railway Works (the south end of the Boiler Shop). **Below:** *Great Western Railway Works staff leaving work.*

Throughout the Shopping Centre historic features dating back to the days of GWR are on display; these range from factory memorabilia such as pieces of original machinery and the giant hooters which used to signal the beginning and end of the working day at the Great Western Engineering Works, to the locomotive which forms the centrepiece of the Food Court. To date, this position beside the diners has been occupied in turn by the record-breaking locomotive The City of Truro and the legendary Hagley Hall, just two of the many great steam locomotives built in Swindon.

It was of course as a manufacturer of steam engines that the town rose to fame during the latter half of the 1800s, although the GWR's original

into one of the new boom towns of the 1980s, and today its residents enjoy excellent modern facilities - none more impressive than its Outlet Centre - and a standard of living well above the national average. All this is in itself a remarkable achievement; but what is even more impressive is the town's success in preserving for posterity so many links with its glorious past, and nowhere is its traditional heritage better represented than in McArthurGlen Designer Outlet Great Western.

purpose in building the engineering works which now house the Outlet Centre was simply to provide a maintenance depot for its Bristol to London line. GWR established itself in Swindon at the beginning of an era of enormous public interest in railways, when the whole nation was very excited by the

*Top: The derelict South Mall and machinery prior to construction. **Above:** The South Mall featuring it's old industrial heritage.*

Record Centre and Gallery, and members of the public are welcome to visit them. The wagon works, a masterpiece of industrial engineering designed by I K Brunel himself, were officially opened on 2nd January 1843. Expansion continued; by the end of the 1870s the site had grown to cover of some 326 acres, and the buildings, which covered 77 acres, included machine shops, fitting shops, boilermakers' shops, painting shops, smiths' shops, tool stores and an erecting shop equipped with hydraulic lifting apparatus. Of these, the boiler shop, tank shop and smithy have survived and are now enjoying a new lease of life as the heart of the Designer Outlet Centre. Originally three separate buildings, they have been imaginatively linked together to create a single retail area. The existing structure of the Grade II listed buildings has been retained, however, and indeed throughout the Centre much original architecture has been incorporated within the design. The great charm and character of Brunel's building has been preserved and enhanced by the addition of modern glazing and other features which complement the original structures perfectly. The centre has the original roof, skylights, arched walls and fretwork cast iron beams; areas of the original brickwork have been left exposed to excellent effect, and the original wood block floor has been sealed and tiled over to preserve it for future generations.

prospect of rail travel and all the opportunities it opened up. Between 1844 and 1850 the country's rail network grew by around 200 per cent, and the GWR's own network expanded steadily, eventually covering the whole of south-west England and much of the West Midlands. More engines and wagons were needed; so, rather than wait for additional rolling stock to be supplied by outside manufacturers, GWR began manufacturing its own wagons at Swindon in 1843, and in February 1846, following major investment in new engineering and workshop facilities, the very first steam engine was built here, a 0-6-0 goods engine named Premier. The following April Swindon's first broad-gauge locomotive, named The Great Western, began trials, and Swindon was poised to make its mark on railway history.

The earliest GWR buildings on the site were the general offices, which included the small office of the first Locomotive Superintendent, Daniel Gooch, and a warehouse. These buildings are now occupied by the National Monuments

BAA McArthurGlen's innovative and ambitious concept of transforming the former GWR workshops into a themed designer retail environment, together with the care with which the entire scheme has been carried out, have won well-deserved praise from many quarters including HRH the Prince of Wales himself. The company, a joint venture between

Above: *The East Mall.*
Right: *A night-time view of the entrance to McArthur Glen.*

leading airport operator BAA and McArthurGlen Europe, has opened eight prestigious designer outlet centres in Britain and Europe since 1995, and has a policy of building and maintaining strong relationships with local towns and communities. In Swindon, BMG worked closely with planning authorities, English Heritage, tourist organisations and local businesses, and has succeeded in created a stimulating retail environment which has simultaneously captured the spirit of the town's past and created new and exciting opportunities for the future.

A hundred years ago, Brunel's engineering works played an important part in the economy of the town, providing employment for over 10,000 men. The peak of GWR's prosperity came in the 1920s when it had 3,858 locomotives covering some 97 million miles a year, the vast majority of them made in Swindon. When in 1960 the appropriately-named Evening Star, the last Swindon-made steam locomotive, brought the era to an end, many local people were devastated at the loss of an industry which had played such an important part in the establishment of the town. It is especially pleasing therefore that the site which was so central to the development and prosperity of the town in the past has found a new and exciting role to play in the economy of the present-day Swindon. Today, the Designer Outlet at Western employs 1,000 people, and some four million people a year - representing a significant contribution to the local economy - visit the former GWR workshop, now a unique setting for more than 100 leading shops, a food court, a children's play area, and a creche; all modern refinements - including air-conditioning, which because of the sheer size of the building posed a particularly interesting challenge - have been incorporated, and there is parking for over 1850 cars and coaches.

McArthurGlen Designer Outlet Great Western has received an impressive list of awards in its first two years. Its inspired architectural design has won recognition in the form of a National Railway Heritage Award 1998, Retail Week's Best Property Award 1998, SEN Retail Magazine's Creativity in Retail - Best Exteriors 1998, and a Civic Trust Award (Commendation) in 1999, while the concept as a whole has been named Best UK Shopping Centre Award 1997 and 1998, Best European Shopping Centre (Commendation) 1998, and Best Visitor Attraction 1998.

Swindon, with its history of innovation and success on a grand scale, can be proud that, thanks to McArthurGlen, both these traditions are continuing in such fine style on the same site. And the innovation is set to continue: at the time of writing, Phase II of this tremendous project is under way, with the old brass shop currently under refurbishment to provide an additional 25,000 square foot of retail space and a further hundred or so jobs. There is no doubt that the GWR Works, now buzzing with activity once again as McArthurGlen Designer Outlet Great Western, is back on track for success.

Below: *The Restaurant featuring a preserved Great Western engine .* ***Bottom:*** *The Children's play area.*

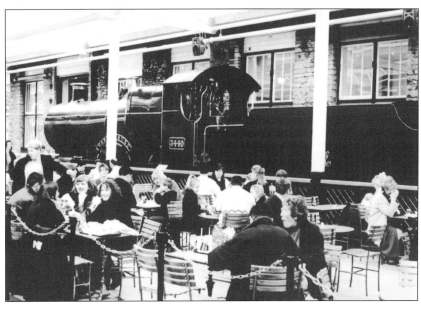

80 years of family funeral service

The only thing certain in life is that it must end. When the day of judgement arrives it is important for all those left behind to feel that the one who has passed over has had a send off that was conducted with care and dignity. The Hillier Funeral Service has been guaranteeing that since the early 1920s. Times and fashion change, but the needs of the deceased's family and friends stay constant. The Hillier family has been engaged in sympathetic, but efficient, service through three generations. When Harold Hillier established the company the dust had only just settled after World War I. He saw service in the Royal Flying Corps, flying De Havilland 9A Bombers. He was born in Swindon in 1900, the same year as Queen Elizabeth, George VI's wife. After his war service he worked for the Great Western Railway. Locals called this 'going inside'. He was

'released' after a short time and established a building company at The Broadway, Rodbourne Cheney. It was in the days when homes fit for heroes had been promised by the government for the brave souls who had survived the horrors of that war that had been supposed to end all wars. Harold did his bit. His workforce of some 60 men built many

Left: *Harold Hillier, founder of the firm.*
Below: *One of the fleet in the early 1930s.*
Bottom: *A 1939 funeral conducted by Hilliers.*

houses in the area and was best known for William Bowles Hall in Cheney Manor Road. But, a black cloud lay on the horizon. The depression days arrived and contracts dried up. His cousin Jack, who had worked as an undertaker, suggested that Harold tried his hand carrying out funerals. For a while, the shrinking building business ran side by side with this new venture.

Needing to develop the funeral service within a larger community, in 1932 an office was set up in a house in Swindon. The workshops, garage and chapel of rest stayed at Broadway. Coffins were prepared by hand from butts of oak or elm that were delivered to the workshop. There they would be sawed and planed into a crafted final resting place for someone's loved one. All this work was done by hand. Local artists engraved the name plate. These days, the coffins are bought from a supplier and the plates engraved on the premises. The first motor hearse was bought in 1933. Before then, funerals were conducted with a hand bier. During World War II many staff members were called up and they were replaced by pensioners. Some work during those dark days involved the American military hospitals,

of which there were several in the area. Hillier's carried out the embalming and preparing of those who died in the hospitals, prior to their being transported to the military cemeteries at Brookwood and Cambridge. For local people, there was no crematorium in the town. One was not opened until 1966. People travelled in the Rolls Royce hearse to Oxford Crematorium as wartime petrol restrictions prohibited such a journey by car.

Harold retired from the business in 1952. He died in 1968. His son, Michael, who had joined the firm in 1944, took over the management. He was more than happy to have the able assistance of Charles Watt in the workshop. He was a cabinet maker who had begun work at Hillier's as a 15 year old. He worked with the company for 55 years. There cannot be many in the country who could claim that level of long service. Harold's grandson, Mark joined the company in 1980 and was in charge when the firm moved to its present address in 1993. His father had retired the year before, though he continued to show an active interest. The new premises offered parking for the seven Volvo vehicles. One of these cost £62,000, considerably more than the £300 paid for the first Austin. There are now four chapels of rest at Rodbourne Cheney and, in 1996, the Hillier Bereavement Care programme was established, providing practical support for the bereaved from qualified counsellors. The Hillier Funeral Service offers a devotion to duty, tact, discretion and that essential we all need - sense of humour when the time is right. The next generation of Hilliers is female and everyone hopes that they will be trend-setters and take over the business one day.

Above: *Michael Hillier.*
Top: *Today's fleet.*
Right: *Mark Hillier.*

One message in a multitude of languages

In these days when there are riots on our streets, wars raging across the world and people having little or no consideration for each other, the message in the Bible becomes more and more important. It is in such times of trouble, whether on a personal or global scale, that we can turn to something that has stood the test of time over two millennia. Fads come and go, but truth is a constant. The Bible acts as a comfort, a reassurance and a guide to all our lives. To follow its teaching is to mark the path along which our lives should run.

Above: Joseph Hughes.
Right: Lord Shaftesbury, who lent his support to the movement.
Below: Queen Victoria Street.

The British and Foreign Bible Society (BFBS) aims to make the Scriptures available to people at a price that is affordable. It also aims to do so in language that they understand; the sort of wording that people use in everyday life, rather than in stuffy prose. It also hopes to give those who are unfamiliar with God's word the chance to get to get to grips with its message. After all, when the Bible was first written, the modern language of the day was used. It is only sensible that everyday language of now is the vehicle that should be used. The BFBS was formed in 1804. It had its origins in the Religious Tract Society and the London Missionary Society. A group of Christians had gathered at a public meeting in a London tavern. There they formed the Society with the intention of providing Bibles, translated into different languages, to other peoples across the world. Originally, the plan had been to translate the Bible into Welsh, for the native

speakers in the Principality. It was the Reverend Joseph Hughes who made the suggestion of an international Bible Society and, so, the BFBS was born.

The idea caught on quickly. Influential people, like Shaftesbury, who had family ties in Purton, and the anti-slavery activist, Wilberforce, lent their support to the movement. They were keen to see the whole world gaining access to the Bible, written in their national mother tongues. It was an era of the foreign missions. As the continents were opened up by intrepid explorers, so missionaries followed in their wake. The first Bible House, in Blackfriars, was opened in 1816. It was the centre of early operations. Within 20 years Bible Societies had been set up across the globe, with London's moral and financial support. In the 1830s a

chain of agents had been established and permanent depots set up. From here travelling salesman, known as 'colporteurs', knocked on doors and encouraged householders far and wide to purchase their own copies of the Bible. They entered market places and anywhere they could get an audience that they could encourage to take the word of God directly into their homes. By World War I there were 1,500 colporteurs working in countries outside the main battle areas. An average of one new language was being added to the list of translations every seven weeks. After World War II, the United Bible Societies was formed. It was set up to co-ordinate the work of the many Bible Societies that then existed.

The house at Blackfriars was compulsorily purchased by the government under a road building scheme and new premises found on Queen Victoria Street. This was the home of the BFBS from 1868 to 1985. It was then that the Swindon connection began. New purpose-built premises were found here. The London site was sold and the profit made meant that funds could be ploughed into increasing and diversifying the work of the BFBS. To-day, the Society, a registered charity, has the Queen and the Queen Mother as its patrons. There are 136 Bible societies working in 200 countries. They now offer Bibles and Bible-related resources in print, on disc, via the internet and on film to give training, information and advice. Congregations and individuals are linked by the word of the Lord.

Above (both pictures): *The Queen Mother opening the Bible Society's premises in 1986.*

The history of the Ridgeway Hospital

Ever since 1843 when Isambard Kingdom Brunel put his engine works in the fields by the old canal, Swindon has been a town of enterprise and vision. The re-building of New Town, the establishment of the commercial centre and the spectacular growth of modern manufacturing demonstrate that that those same qualities still flourish.

And not just amongst the businessmen and politicians either. In the early 1980s, a group of doctors from the local hospital, realised that, if Swindon was to grow, it would need its own independent hospital. They had the vision and the enterprise to use their skills and those of the local business community to build something unique. The company they formed was the only one to be started under the, then available, Business Expansion Scheme at the same time as being floated on the Unlisted Securities Market. The stability afforded by this unique arrangement gave the fledgling hospital five years in which to establish itself in, what was then, a very difficult market.

Below: *Ridgeway Hospital before the opening in June 1984.*

Brenda McLeod, from London, was the hospital's first Matron and John Raggett, from Swindon, its first Director. Both took up their posts on the 1st of March 1984. Although Brenda had many years' clinical experience and was a wonderful nurse, John had never worked in a hospital before, his background was one of hotel and commercial management, seasoned with five years' experience as a detective officer on the Wiltshire Constabulary Fraud Squad.

This unique mixture brought a fresh approach to everything that was done and the atmosphere was one of excellence, innovation and pioneering excitement. The Ridgeway Hospital opened with 40 beds in June 1984. Brenda left after its first year but not before establishing the very highest standards of nursing care which are maintained to this day. John stayed until 1991 but many of the key staff still remain from those early days to carry on what was started then.

Activity within the hospital continued to increase significantly and in 1992 extra accommodation was brought on to the site. Purpose built portacabins were sited to accommodate the Finance and Physio-

therapy departments, thereby increasing consultancy room space in the Outpatients department. During the following year a further cabin was erected to facilitate extra storage space required.

The closure of the RAF Princess Alexandra Hospital, Wroughton in 1995 attracted several RAF Consultant Surgeons to stay and work locally. The Orthopaedic Consultants, in particular attracting patients from the sporting fields, including athletes, football league clubs and the nearby horse racing fraternity.

Plans were submitted to extend The Ridgeway Hospital to meet the growing demand for accommodation. In 1997 when the hospital was acquired by BMI Healthcare, part of the General Healthcare

Group, this major project was agreed and building commenced in the summer of 1998 to provide a High Dependency Unit, a Comprehensive Physiotherapy and Rehabilitation Department including a hydrotherapy pool. The introduction of the first Open Magnetic Resonance Imaging Scanner, in this part of England, and a dedicated Day Care Unit and an extension of the bed capacity to 50 patients. Improvements were also made to the Ward and Theatre area with a Pharmacy being introduced within the Reception area for both Inpatient and Outpatient services. The temporary accommodation will be a thing of the past upon completion of the project.

The Ridgeway Hospital has established a reputation for the provision of quality care to patients, and now provides an important role in the provision of healthcare to the population of Swindon and district. Looking to the future - on completion of the major building project in 1999 - plans were already being drawn up for future developments on the site for the new millennium.

Above left: *The Mayor of Thamesdown, Mrs Doreen Dart, tries the comfort of a bed during her annual Christmas visit in 1995 accompanied by Mr Nigel Harris, the Chief Executive of Amicus Healthcare, Sister Helen Cecil and Hospital Director, Mrs Sheila Maslin.*
Top: *Ridgeway Hospital as it was in 1998.*

It has been a long haul from the fruit stall

The power of the huge trucks used by hauliers to-day makes light of the puny lorries that went before them. A large Volvo of the William Hughes (Swindon) Ltd firm of haulage contractors can manage a load of 24 tons. Compare that with the tiny load of less than 10 per cent managed by the trucks in the 1920s. In the days of the horse and cart, at the beginning of the 20th century, only a tiny fraction of that amount could have been handled. In 1900, one horse power meant exactly that. As someone once said, 'Size matters'. Certainly it does in this line of business. The more you can move, the less there is to be stored or to be left awaiting transportation. A greater volume can be handled and a quicker turn round of business achieved. However, you need more garage space for your vehicles and more warehouse room for supplies that have stockpiled. There are swings and roundabouts in commerce, just as everywhere else.

Life is certainly different from that of 100 years ago. It is more than that. It is a completely different world we live in - different values, different pace and different skills. That was when the three Hughes brothers set up a retail and wholesale business in Bath, selling fruit and vegetables. There was no

Volvo for them to use to get to and from the markets and suppliers. It was a mixture of Shanks' pony and their own horse and cart. Many others plied similar trades from their barrows around the town and the air was filled with the cries of the barrow boys and stallholders on market day. The air was filled with calls advertising the produce for sale. 'Only a halfpenny for a pound of apples' or 'You won't get finer anywhere else' could be heard as potential customers were encouraged to part with their hard earned cash. In 1914, another cry came across even louder. It was Lord Kitchener telling us that 'Your country needs you'. Albert Hughes heard the call and went off to France to do his bit for King and country. On demob he settled in Swindon and continued in the line of business he had started before the war. It was in Regent Street that the cries of the fruit and veg salesman could be heard once more. It is ironic to discover the next major event in the Hughes family history. Having come through the bloodiest war that the world had known and lived to tell the tale, Albert was to come to a sad and wasteful end. A sudden

Above: Hughes Bros stall in Bath Market.
Below: Hughes delivery vehicles and their drivers circa 1926.

noise or shout startled his horse into bolting. Albert was standing on the back of the cart, totally unprepared for the sudden movement. He was thrown to the ground and fatally injured.

Brother William, known as Bill to everyone, brought the business from Albert's widow. He began trading in 1920 as W Hughes. Bill installed a fellow Bath colleague, Sid Bristow, as manager. The firm moved to larger premises on Cromwell Street in the mid 1920s. There was a warehouse behind the retail shop and at this time the trusty horse and cart gave way to the first of the motor vehicles that were to become the centre of the business in years to come. Throughout the next dozen years or so the firm ticked over very nicely, without any major change. It was left to Herr Hitler to do that. As the war dragged on, fresh fruit was in short supply. There were few imports and Bill and Sid had to rely on the locals who were digging for victory. Fortunately, there was a plentiful supply of locally grown vegetables and the army camps in the area were eager customers for supplies to their canteens. Soldiers on jankers were not too happy when they saw the potato wagon on

its way. That meant more spud bashing, but Bill and Sid were happy to keep the business going. Sid retired at the end of the war and was replaced by Len Ricketts. In 1949, Bill's grandson, Geoffrey, joined the firm. Like the other family members, his home was in Bath and he usually commuted from there. In busier times he would stay overnight at one of the local hotels.

Business increased under the guidance of Geoff Hughes. W Hughes became the limited company of William Hughes (Swindon) in 1959. By 1964, it had outgrown the Cromwell Street premises. Cromwell Street is no more, having given way to urban redevelopment. A new warehouse was built at Marshgate, from where the company still operates. Business was really booming. Bigger and better

Top left: *Will Junior, left, and Bill Senior together in the late 1920s.* ***Below:*** *A Bedford OB from 1949 which nowadays competes at Vintage Vehicle shows throughout the country and is also used by film and television companies.*
Right: *Mr Hughes being presented with a trophy which the Bedford OB won in 1995.*

vehicles covered a larger area. When not needed for fruit movements, some of the lorries were involved in haulage, a sign of things to come. By the end of the 1970s, Geoff recognised that the threat of the supermarket had become very real. As its influence grew, so the small time greengrocer was being squeezed, along with those connected in supply and transport. Geoff received an offer from a large fruit distributor to buy out the business and he was contracted to integrate the business with another smaller one on a larger site. Many of his former

employees went with him, but one, Bob Hatcher, stayed at Marshgate. He ran a small haulage operation from part of the premises, the remaining space being leased by a fruit and flowers wholesaler. The haulage business expanded and most of the building was returned to the Hughes company before too long. On completion of his contract with the fruit distributor, Geoff returned to work with Bob. Since then the business has continued to expand. There are now 14 vehicles rolling in and out of Stratton Road, proudly showing their red and white colours as they serve their customers. These include printers. packaging manufacturers and

recyclers of plastics. The client base has been established on a business philosophy of keeping the customer happy. Providing a personal service that can offer speedy and reliable reactions to client needs, William Hughes Ltd has built a well merited reputation through three generations of the family. Whilst hoping to continue to grow a little more, it is a firm that is still happy to serve.

Above: *One of the 14 vehicles that William Hughes Ltd operates today.* ***Top:*** *W Hughes fruit delivery lorries line up outside the Cromwell Street premises in 1954.*

Swindon - home to the top Society

windon has been the home of the Nationwide Building Society since 1974. Four years earlier the London-based Co-Operative Permanent Building Society changed its name to Nationwide Building Society and began looking for a site for another administration centre. It chose Princes Street in Swindon; and when after two decades of growth larger premises were needed, the Society was so settled in the town that it acquired a greenfield site in Pipers Way. The new administration centre was officially opened in April 1992, and that same year it also became the new head office. Since then Nationwide's links with the town have strengthened still more; the Society plays an active role in the community in the form of charitable donations, selected sponsorships and staff fund-raising efforts. It is also the main sponsor of the England football team - although locally it is its support of Swindon Town Football Club which is particularly appreciated!

Essentially the role of the building society has changed little over the past 150 years. The building society movement began in the 1770s, when workers clubbed together and saved, through regular contributions, for land and materials with which to build houses of their own; when each member had a house the society was wound up. By the 1880s, however, many societies were becoming the permanent home-loans and savings institutions which are familiar to us today.

The Nationwide originally grew out of the Northampton Town and County Building Society (founded in 1848) and the Co-Operative movement (established in London in 1833). Today, after over a hundred mergers - notably with Anglia Building Society in 1987 - Nationwide is the largest building society in the UK and offers a broad range of financial services including mortgages, savings, current accounts, life assurance, investment products, personal loans and household insurance. It is committed to putting members first by providing a full range of top value, quality financial services that are widely available and delivered with speed, courtesy and reliability; and because it intends to remain a building society, it can work towards long-term benefits for its members, rather than short-term benefits for shareholders.

Today's Nationwide members can take advantage of automated teller machines (ATMs), PC Home banking and branch-based self-service multimedia technology to access their money and conduct their business with the Society. But while the technology in Nationwide's Regent Street branch in Swindon - one of the latest generation of branches - would have astonished an aspiring homebuyer of the mid 19th century, the good old-fashioned customer service would have been just what they expected.

Above: *The Founding Fathers from the Northampton Town and County Building Society.*
Below: *Nationwide House, Nationwide's head office in Pipers Way, Swindon.*

The oldest home for the youngest at heart

None of us is getting any younger, you know. Of course we know. It is one of the facts of life. As medical science improves and we look after our bodies better by eating and exercising sensibly, then the saying will perhaps change to, 'We are all getting older, you know'. certainly, we are living longer than our parents and Britain is fast becoming a state with a large percentage of pensioners to be funded and then cared for in extreme old age or infirmity. The Cheriton Nursing Home has had experience of caring for the elderly longer than any other such Home in Swindon. It can be found in the old part of the town. There are lovely views across the Marlborough Downs and it is delightful just to sit and relax in the gardens and let the world go by. For the more energetic, there are the popular Town Gardens nearby.

The nursing home, consisting of two Victorian houses, owned by Miss Woolcott, was in business here circa 1918. Eight doctors, Dr Robert Beatty, Dr Donald Cameron, Dr William DeLacey, Dr Jeremiah Holland, Dr W Thomas May, Dr Samuel McDermott, Dr Thomas Quigley and Mr James Scholfield, who were in local practices and also involved with the Great Western and Victoria Hospitals, purchased The Cheriton in 1947.

From then until the early 1960s, as well as providing general nursing care the doctors incorporated an operating theatre and maternity unit into their services at the Home. Often, residents of Swindon are pleased to tell us that they were born at The Cheriton. When Princess Margaret Hospital opened The Cheriton became dedicated to the care of the elderly.

The current owners/directors, who are the second and third generations of Dr Cameron, Dr May and Dr McDermott, have upheld the aim of the founder/directors that The Cheriton provides a service to the people of Swindon. Mary Butler, who managed the Home for over thirty years, was appointed to the Board of Directors in 1987. All the directors are very much involved in the Home. Over the years as Swindon has expanded, The Cheriton has also grown and now occupies six Victorian houses and is still very much dedicated to the Care of the Elderly in Swindon.

Above left: *Dr Thomas May, a founder director of Cheriton, pictured here with some of the nurses.*
Below: *Resident Gladys Dallman's 100th birthday celebrations in 1998.* ***Bottom:*** *Cheriton Nursing Home's grounds today.*

The hotel in the centre of community life

Those taking a short break at the Blunsdon House Hotel will wish that their stay was even longer. There is so much to do and enjoy. As part of the Best Western group, it boasts leisure facilities to suit young and old, big and small. Those seeking a tone up will enjoy the well equipped gymnasiums, saunas and steam rooms. The more energetic can rush around the tennis and squash courts or practise their sand wedge technique from the devilish bunkers that decorate the nine hole golf course. A woodland walk, with its delightful countryside views, is a peaceful way to work up an appetite for dinner in either of the excellent restaurants. Kiddies enjoy splashing in their pool or having fun in the adventure playground. There is something for everyone.

Overlooking the Vale of Crickade, Blunsdon House Hotel was a private house for 150 years before becoming a hotel in 1957. It had been built as a hunting lodge on the St Leonard's Farm estate. In Victorian times the house was an imposing sight to the members of the rural community who lived nearby. Large gateposts at the entrance to the circular drive guided you to a sweeping vista that took in conifers, evergreen shrubs, flower gardens and climbing plants that decorated the house's Georgian style facade. At the start of the 20th century, the house had become the centre of village celebrations. There were Sunday School tea parties and village treats on the lawn. Cricket matches, country dancing and donkey rides were a source of joy to the locals. When Peter and Zan Clifford began the hotel business at Blunsdon House, they vowed to continue the philosophy of providing a hotel that was as much a part of community life as it was a commercial enterprise. Their son, John, has seen that it continues to hold true to those principles. Not surprisingly, locals are keen to use the facilities for their conferences, wedding receptions and special evenings. Discos, line dancing and cookery classes are amongst the varied events on offer. There are no half measures in providing a pleasurable service.

Above left: *The house circa 1885.*
Below: *Outside catering - 1960s style.*
Bottom: *The hotel in 1964.*

This photograph shows the site of the old canal, providing convenient parking for shopping in Regent Street.

Acknowledgements

Swindon Borough Council Libraries

Thanks are also due to
Margaret Wakefield who penned the editorial text and
Andrew Mitchell for his copywriting skills